Your New Name

SAYING GOODBYE TO THE
LABELS THAT LIMIT

ESTHER FLEECE ALLEN

ZONDERVAN

ZONDERVAN

Your New Name
Copyright © 2020 by Esther Fleece Allen

Requests for information should be addressed to:
Zondervan, *3900 Sparks Dr. SE, Grand Rapids, Michigan 49546*

Zondervan titles may be purchased in bulk for educational, business, fundraising, or promotional use. For information, please email SpecialMarkets@Zondervan.com.

ISBN 978-0-310-34607-4 (softcover)

ISBN 978-0-310-35567-0 (audio)

ISBN 978-0-310-34608-1 (ebook)

The author is represented by the literary agency of Alive Literary Agency, www.alive literary.com.

Cover design: James W. Hall IV
Cover photo: Giada Canu / Stocksy
Interior design: Kait Lamphere

Printed in the United States of America

20 21 22 23 24 25 26 27 28 29 30 /LSC/ 15 14 13 12 11 10 9 8 7 6 5 4 3 2 1

It's easy to get a little confused about who we are. This book is a gentle reminder from a voice I trust, to stop letting other people decide who you are and let Jesus name you.

BOB GOFF, author of the *New York Times* bestsellers *Love Does* and *Everybody, Always*

This book is a much-needed reminder of how powerful and prophetic names can be. Esther Fleece Allen beautifully illustrates the gift we have as children of God, what this sacred identity means, and why this gift is so precious and powerful. I read this book while pregnant with my third child, and I will never look at naming a child the same way again. I recommend *Your New Name* wholeheartedly!

MEGAN ALEXANDER, correspondent for *Inside Edition* and author of *Faith in the Spotlight*

In a world that wants to quickly size us up and define us by our past, our status, our title, and even our outward appearances, Esther Fleece Allen beautifully shows us the power of our true identity—an identity that never changes, never fades, and never disappoints. If you can grab hold of the truths in this book, fear and insecurity will lose their grip on you. You will have the courage and authenticity to live life fully and freely, without fear of the past or anxiety about the future.

VALORIE BURTON, bestselling author of *Successful Women Think Differently* and *It's About Time*

In the follow-up to *No More Faking Fine*, Esther Fleece Allen has again woven more of her incredible story and pastoral heart into a theological exegesis that reminds us what names and labels should be the ones we let speak the loudest. This is a Bible-study memoir worth reading to see the names you respond to, the labels you give others, and what God has to say about it all.

DR. EMERSON EGGERICHS, founder and president of Love and Respect Ministries and author of *The 4 Wills of God*

Everything changes when we believe and lean into who God says we are. *Your New Name* is a beautiful tool to help us do just that.

LEVI LUSKO, lead pastor of Fresh Life
Church and bestselling author

With wisdom and a beautiful heart, Esther Fleece Allen helps us see that who we are isn't what we do or where we've been; it's in God's redefining. No to labels; yes to a new name and inviting in freedom.

LISA WHITTLE, Bible teacher,
author, and podcast host of
Jesus Over Everything

Esther Fleece Allen calls believers to walk in the strength and hope of their God-given identity and does so with great depth, compassion, and richness of biblical teaching that we find restorative. This book shines with the love and healing only our beautiful Messiah makes possible. Read it, and may your heart of worship and knowledge of God grow tenfold!

JOEL AND LYNN ROSENBERG,
New York Times bestselling author and
cofounders of The Joshua Fund

Your New Name is a fantastic display of God's love and transformational power. From the time of our birth until our death, we are told who we are or who we're supposed to be. What I love about Esther Fleece Allen's book is how she clearly shares who God has called us to be and, equally important, how God views us, despite our past failures and titles. If you're in an identity crisis and looking for encouragement, look no further than *Your New Name*.

REMI ADELEKE, author of *Transformed*,
actor, and former Navy SEAL

Esther Fleece Allen gives such a beautiful reminder of how secure and powerful it is to be a child of God. Our identity in Jesus is full of the purest truth, is always secure, and is never-changing. It's easy to label ourselves based on what we have been through or what we have accomplished, and Esther uses her story and the Bible to remind us of the importance to stand firm in who God says we are. Resting in this truth is life-changing.

LAUREN SCRUGGS KENNEDY, founder of
LSK, The Lauren Scruggs Kennedy Foundation,
and *New York Times* bestselling author

Believing we are who God says we are is so hard in our world today. Esther Fleece Allen calls us to look toward God to find our truest identity and in so doing to find the freedom to live out of who we are called to be.

JAY AND KATHERINE WOLF, authors
of *Hope Heals* and *Suffer Strong*

Your New Name came at a poignant time for me. For months, I had been thinking about the significance of a name and the powerful message that is sent when we choose to call someone by their name. Written with the authentic and refreshingly real voice that is Esther Fleece Allen, this book uniquely reaches each reader as it calls to each of us by name. Esther drew me into a vulnerable place of asking the question "What is my great fear, and how has God specifically called to me in response?" I immediately heard one word: *Enough.* Could it be that a name my God calls me is "Enough." I urge you to remember the value of the earthly name bestowed on you that speaks to an identity like no other. And allow Esther to show you that this is but the beginning, for your identity is ultimately found in Christ. In a beautiful way, God doesn't bypass a name. No, He affirms both who you are and who He created you to be. And you will want to lift your head to answer as He calls you by name.

NAOMI ZACHARIAS, director of Wellspring
International and author of *The Scent of Water*

Names matter! They are a major part of our identity in this world. The apostle Paul tells us in 2 Corinthians 5:17 that through Christ we become a new creation, allowing us to have a new name. If you're ready to leave behind the labels you've been given or have given yourself and step into your God-given name, then start reading this book now.

JACKIE GREEN, cofounder of Museum
of the Bible and coauthor of *Only One
Life* and *This Dangerous Book*

To my husband, Joel Chandler Allen.
Thank you for choosing me, loving me,
and giving me a new name.
I love you.

Contents

Foreword

I met Esther a decade ago in the greenroom of the Catalyst conference. She was a cheerful, friendly person, well-respected, and everyone seemed to know her. A clear extrovert, she sat down next to me and thanked me for a recent sermon series that spoke to her. I quickly learned Esther is a natural connector, who is respected by people of various backgrounds, denominations, and religions.

More than a decade later, Esther's name is still respected. She is a leader. She crosses spheres of influence to reconcile theological camps that haven't previously gotten along. She breaks down barriers to facilitate conversations that lead to real relationships. Where previous generations may have labeled someone "guilty by association," Esther seeks to know people's names and stories, all in an effort to reflect the God who has given her a new name.

Esther's motivation can be our motivation—that in Christ we become new, and this newness is meant to be shared with the world. While previously we were once far off, we have been brought near to God by the blood of Christ.

God makes us into a new person, and living out of this newness is what tears down the wall of hostility that previously divided generations, ethnicities, denominations, and more.

The apostle Paul writes in Ephesians 2:13–16 (emphasis mine), "In Christ Jesus you who once were far away have been brought near by the blood of Christ. For he himself is our peace, who has made the two groups *one* and has destroyed the barrier, the dividing wall of hostility . . . His purpose was to create in himself *one new humanity* out of the two, thus making peace, and in *one* body to reconcile both of them to God through the cross, by which he put to death their hostility."

Some of us focus only on being reconciled to God, forgetting our call to reconcile to one another. Others of us put all of our time and attention into making peace with others, forgetting to know God personally and reconcile to Him in the process. But our faith calls us to a both/and commitment. God gives us a new name so that we can live new and reflect new.

Esther has tapped into something significant in this book that will help us live out our Christian faith. When we live out of our new names, we can approach God boldly. When we know *who* we belong to, we can seek out relationship with others. When our identity is firmly planted in who God says we are, we can throw off the labels that limit us and do away with the name-calling that is rampant throughout the world.

When God saves us, He doesn't stick us into a mold like labels do. God saves us and makes us into someone *new*. Living out of our new name is the very thing that will break down the walls of hostility that have existed between us for far too long.

Your new name is meant to put God's name on display. Living out of our new name is our best chance for becoming one. That is my prayer for you as you journey through this book: that you will experience the difference and the power of living out of the name God has for you.

Andy Stanley, bestselling author and founder
and pastor at North Point Ministries

Note to Reader

Dear reader,

Life can be weighty, and you can feel stuck. While your circumstances may make you numb, I wrote this book with the great hope that you will know that God cares to make things right for you. God knows you, thinks of you, helps you, and rebuilds you so that you can endure. Discovering your new name is the next step forward after being in a season of lament.

My first book, *No More Faking Fine*, addressed a hard spiritual season in my life. I felt like either I had failed God or He had forgotten about me—and either way, it was causing me to lose hope and confidence. I had lost sight of *who* I was and *whose* I was.

But lament was not the end of my story, and it won't be the final song for you either. Your new name does not come by your deeds, good or bad, or your scars. God has a new name for you that is not determined by your successes or failures. Have you asked Him for it? Your new name is not based on your job title, your net worth, your health, or your relationship status. Your new name reflects who God is, and it will stay with you throughout eternity.

No matter what spiritual season you're in, I pray this book will help rebuild your faith in the God of grace. After you have suffered a little while, God will restore you. God is all about new beginnings, new seasons, and new names.

And my prayer for you is that today will be a beautiful beginning of living out of your new name.

Esther Fleece Allen

PART 1

So What's in a Name?

CHAPTER 1

How You Get a New Name

Therefore, if anyone is in Christ, the new creation has
come: The old has gone, the new is here!
2 CORINTHIANS 5:17

Our names are the most essential thing about us. It's often the first thing people know about us, and yet this one word holds far more significance and sacred history than any first impression could ever capture.

My name is Esther, and like every name, mine has a story.

In 1937, a film debuted featuring a musician who discovers a talented younger singer, only to later fall in love with her. This story line was so popular that it later became a musical and then a rock musical and then a Bollywood romantic film. This movie was remade again in 2018, and it featured Lady Gaga and Bradley Cooper. The 1976 version of the movie *A Star Is Born* starred Kris Kristofferson as a rock-and-roll star and Barbra Streisand as the lead actress, who was named Esther. I was told that this is where my name, Esther, came from. My biological mom saw the name

Esther in this movie and decided it was the name for me. So in 1982, Esther Marion Fleece was born.

Esther means "star," which is where the movie title *A Star Is Born* came from. I never told people this was where my name was from, because I was kind of embarrassed. My name didn't seem to have much meaning beyond a blockbuster movie, and it didn't feel personal to me.

Yet my name makes me distinct, and your name makes you distinct.

Our names help people in our communities set us apart and see us as individuals. Someone shouting, "Hey, you!" across the street can sure feel impersonal. But when a neighbor addresses us by our name, we pay attention and feel seen. We feel respected when someone remembers our name. It's such a simple gift, yet it creates such a strong impression.

Have you ever had your name pronounced wrong at the Starbucks counter and found yourself annoyed? Or do you have a name that's consistently tricky for others to get right? We may feel angry or sad or disappointed when our names are mispronounced, misspelled, misused, laughed at, minimized, or forgotten.

There is One, though, who knows your name and knows the true you.

Your name is known by God. Even if your earthly name feels random or insignificant, it is precious to God. He wants you to understand the meaning of your given name, and—even more importantly—He wants to give you a new name and identity.

Are you ready to hear it?

THE LOST ART OF NAMING

Sometimes I think we've lost the art of naming in our culture. I've found that the names we choose for our kids have a lot to do with the culture and generation in which we were raised. We choose names we like, names that flow together, and names that pair well with our last name. We consult baby name books and lists, looking for trends and unique options that will set our child apart.

But sometimes I wonder if there's more to naming than sounds and syllables.

Are we settling for a smaller version of what our names mean and the power they hold?

In the ancient world, names were given to reflect who a person was or who they were to become. A lot of names had the name of God woven into them. "El" is a word for God that is often incorporated into the biblical names for God. The most common name for God in Scripture is "Elohim," appearing more than two thousand times. We hear this "el" syllable in a number of the human names we read in Scripture, like Daniel ("God is my Judge") and Nathaniel ("gift of God").

Moving to the New Testament, we see names still bearing significance but also being chosen to honor a family member. Many of our homes carry on this tradition today, as children are named to honor a parent or grandparent. But many of us don't know what our name really means or why our parents chose it for us. Many of us were named according to what was popular at the time, more than for the significance the word itself bears.

And if we're not aware of the very first word spoken over our lives, are we missing out? Are we missing the gift of pressing into the meaning of our name and living it out?

We are told that words have the power of life and death (Proverbs 18:21), and so does living out of the right name.

If we take a look at the Bible, we see that God pays a lot of attention to naming things. God brings things into existence by naming them.

> Lift up your eyes and look to the heavens:
> Who created all these?
> He who brings out the starry host one by one
> and calls forth each of them by name.
>
> ISAIAH 40:26

Can you imagine God caring so much about names that He even names the stars?

God also named the first human, Adam. He calls Adam and Eve "mankind" (Genesis 1:26–27) and then gives Adam the task of naming the animals (Genesis 2:20).

Adam was also given the task of naming his wife. What a privilege it was to name the second human being! God wanted people, animals, stars, and creatures to have names, and He allowed Adam to name his wife (Genesis 3:20).

Because human parents commonly name children, we may take this privilege for granted. But it's significant that the first human, made in the image of God and named by God, was told to name things. This is the authority we have when we name our children and even our animals. We are made in the image of God and are invited to participate in naming people and things, just like He does.

Names establish uniqueness and display value. And knowing our names, as well as what they mean, helps us walk in the confidence that we are known, are chosen, and belong.

Think of a woman who is pregnant and preparing for the birth of her child. Naming her child is one of the first tasks she considers. Where the child will go to school, who their friends will be, and what sports they will play can wait, but a name happens first. When a child's name is selected and registered, their identity will be confirmed by the government through their social security number. Naming someone confirms their place here on earth. It's why some parents who choose to name a preborn baby say that

knowing their name helps make the experience "more real" for
them as they wait to meet their child.

Names *matter*.

NAMES REVEAL VALUE
AND MEANING

For years, I didn't really know the significance of the name that
had been chosen for me. Similarly, I'm afraid we have lost the significance of naming in our culture today. Many of us don't appre-
ciate the power inherent in names that confer meaning and value.

That wasn't true of those we meet in the biblical story. The
vast majority of the time, the meaning of a name in the Bible
was significant. Some names, like Uzziah (2 Chronicles 26), were
a creedal statement: "Yahweh is my strength." Other names,
like Joshua, made a statement about God: "Yahweh is salvation."
Some names functioned as prophecy (Hosea 1:4–11), and some
were familial or spoke to physical circumstances. Many biblical
accounts explain the meaning of a person's name, and those names
were significant to who those individuals were or who they were
to become.

In Jewish tradition, a child's name was revealed in the same
ceremony in which they were circumcised, a sign of the covenant.
God's ancient people knew that a good name is to be esteemed
more than silver or gold (Proverbs 22:1).

One of my best friends, Sally, named her son Cross. To this
day, it is one of my favorite boy names. Sally knows the value of
the cross and the price Jesus paid for us through His death and
resurrection. As a mom with the power and authority to name,
she chose the name Cross so that her son's name would speak of
the most important event in human history. Cross's name is an
example of how a name can carry weight and meaning.

Maybe you weren't assigned an awesome name like Cross's at your birth but were given a pretty remarkable and meaningful name when you became God's child.

When we become followers of Christ, God makes each one of us a new creation (2 Corinthians 5:17). He has made us to be ministers of a new covenant (2 Corinthians 3:6). Often this newness is evident in our lives. We are empowered to pursue new life in Christ. He helps us clean up our language and make it new. God cleans up our hearts and makes them new. In many areas—from relationships to the ways we use money—we release the old way of doing things and embrace a new way. We understand what it means to be made into new people, but rarely do we pay attention to our new name.

Did you know that all of us who are in Christ have been given a new name? When we become a Christian, we immediately bear Christ's name. Luke teaches that "the disciples were called Christians first at Antioch" (Acts 11:26). Later in the first century, Christians were called followers of "the Way" (Acts 9:2).

The word often translated "new" in the New Testament is the Greek word *kainos,* and it means "new and fresh." HELPS Word-studies tells us that *kainos* means "fresh in development or opportunity—because 'not found exactly like this before.'"[1] Some of us hear that when we are in Christ, we become new creations (2 Corinthians 5:17), or we look forward to the new bodies we will get in heaven (2 Corinthians 5:2). Or we are familiar with the term "new covenant" (Jeremiah 31:31; Hebrews 8:13; 9:15; Luke 22:20), found in both the Old and New Testaments. But why isn't anyone talking about our new name?

When we know our new name, we are remade as we live into the power of that name, and we're no longer identified by the circumstances we've come from. We are made new as we're reidentified by our relationship to God, and along with that comes a new name.

While a label can group us with other people, an individual name sets us apart. There may be fifteen hundred or fifteen thousand people who work at your company or organization, but your name badge, your email address, and your paycheck confirm that you are you. While you may share a name with others, your name is part of who you are and makes you distinct.

Many of us have incorrectly taken on labels as our names. Maybe we have been labeled a "loser" or a "dropout" or "unemployed." Maybe we've labeled ourselves "unattractive" or "overweight" or "undesirable." But God doesn't settle for labels that limit. Instead, He gives us names that call us into a new identity that He has crafted just for us—names with meanings and names that speak to who we will become. God sees us individually, has good plans for us individually, and wants us to have a distinct name, purpose, and calling. I wonder if mislabeling yourself has prevented you from knowing your new name.

What is most true about us is that when we become Christ followers, we take on the new name of "Son" or "Daughter." God planned our adoption as sons and daughters through Jesus Christ, and it was His pleasure and will to do so (Ephesians 1:5). This means that if you are a follower of Jesus, you are a child of God with a new name. To all of us who receive God, and to those of us who believe in His name, He gives the right to become children of God (John 1:12). Previously I was an orphan, but now I have the name of "Adopted." I exchanged the label "orphan" for the new name of "Daughter," and it has made a world of difference.

It takes time to learn to live out of our new names, and there are more names for us than "Son" or "Daughter." Some followers of God in the Bible were renamed completely—Abram to Abraham, Sarai to Sarah, Jacob to Israel. A few of us may receive a new name in that way, and we'll take a look at their stories throughout the book. Others of us may keep our physical name while receiving a new spiritual name that empowers us to live the life God has for us to live.

Some of us will be renamed according to who God is calling us to become. Some folks in the Bible were being called to live into their new identities as followers of Jesus. Men like Andrew, James, and John received not a new physical name but a new identity when they were called away from fishing for fish to fishing for people (Matthew 4:19). Others—like Simon, whose name became Peter—received a new name. What is consistent is that after they met Jesus, they were known as "Fishers of People," and this spiritual name changed how they lived here on earth.

Beyond the shared names that God gives to everyone in His family and the names we get when we partner in the mission of God, God also gives names that are unique to our personal circumstances.

God assigns us new names to replace the old labels we once wore. To the one who was called ugly, God gives the name "Beauty." To the one who was ignored, He gives the name "Seen and Heard." To the one who was rejected, God gives the name "Chosen." To the one who was a victim, He gives the name "Overcomer."

How about you? What were you before you met Christ? Were you a rebel? Were you mistreated? Were you suffering? Were you forgotten? What labels have limited your life? What false names assigned by others have held you back?

If you don't know yet, that's okay. I've prayed that you will discover any new name that God has for you as you read and finish this book. There's no pressure on you, because this new name is given, not earned. Your new name has value, even before you recognize or become aware of it, because of the One who gives it to you. So relax. You can receive a new name from God in a variety of ways you'll discover in these pages.

God's name for you is not some elusive secret that only "super" Christians figure out in this life. No, God's name for you is the truest thing about you. It is core to your very identity. Your name may be several names that God speaks throughout Scripture. Knowing your new name makes it personal to you. For every label that limits you, God speaks your true name.

Maybe you've been told you're shy or introverted, and this has made you unhappy about the way you engage with others. God may want to encourage you that the way He has wired you is not a mistake. Maybe you've felt chained by your past, but God wants to name you "Free Indeed." Or maybe you've struggled to feel like you belong. God may want to name you His "Beloved Child" and affirm to you that the applause of others is not an indication of His pleasure with you.

Learning our new names isn't always about receiving a divine word through some mystical experience; rather it more often than not is about learning to trust the voice of God that has been speaking over our lives all along.

And I want you to hear that these names are for *every* child of God. Perhaps you feel like you don't deserve a new name because you haven't walked perfectly with God, but that is *not* God's voice. God is constantly in the business of making us new. We will be called many names here on earth, but it's important to reflect on whose voice we are listening to. Have you taken time to listen to what God says about you?

There are many labels in life that limit us—labels assigned to us by our circumstances, our past, our deficiencies, the things others say about us, the backgrounds we come from, and the lies we believe. We'll look at many of these labels throughout the book to help you identify what you are not, because no matter who you are or what kind of life you've lived, *God has a new name for you.*

You may be seventy or even eighty years old and feel like you've missed the opportunity to be renamed. Not so. God is always wanting to do a new and fresh thing inside us, and it's never too late for a new identity or a new name in God. New names and words are available to us as God's children—at any and every point in our walk with Christ—and we can know them, access them, and live out of them.

BECOMING ESTHER ALLEN

Some years ago, when I'd been accepted into the business program at the Oxford Centre for Christian Apologetics, I left my job to begin a semester studying in Oxford, England.

My first meal in Oxford was a spaghetti dinner with Jason and Tamy Elam, friends who had become family. This couple had taken me in during my college years and treated me like a family member. They had recently taken their six children to Oxford so Jason could pursue additional studies at the Oxford Centre for Christian Apologetics. They were there to pick me up when I landed, and I was looking forward to spending another season of life with this family I had come to know and love for more than ten years.

Jason had a long and successful career in the National Football League and tried regularly to set me up with friends and teammates. While I appreciated this, I was always too shy to date—though too guarded and unhealed is probably a more accurate way to describe it. And so a decade into our friendship (familyship), Jason knew that telling me he had someone in mind for me would probably cause me to run in the opposite direction. In fact, my nickname in the family became "Gazelle," as I ran fast from the opportunity to be known intimately

Following our nice long catch-up over a spaghetti dinner, the Elams had a friend casually drop by and join us for dessert. This was unexpected to me, but not surprising. Jason has friends all over the world, and I figured this was just another friend (or fan) joining our meal.

I looked up from the red-and-white-checkered tablecloth as we gazed at our dessert menus and saw a tall man standing at the end of the table. He had dark hair and a gleam in his eyes. He looked about my age, but by the way he carried himself, he seemed far more sophisticated than someone in his early thirties. His black suit with a red power tie made me think he was a politician. He had just come from listening to a speech at the Oxford Union, and he introduced himself with a humble Texas accent.

Who is this man? I thought to myself.

I was intrigued, but not interested. I felt uncomfortable when Jason told him my name. I've always been far too embarrassed about my name—because I always thought it sounded like an "old" name for a young woman. On the inside, I was also ashamed of my story and quite sure that no one in their right mind would be interested in me.

This man, Joel, sat down at our table and pulled out his phone. Immediately he began showing us pictures of his new nephew, a recently adopted family member. As someone who was physically and emotionally adopted by a number of families growing up, I have always held adoption close to my heart. Within minutes, I could tell that Joel's heart for family was genuine. Not only did this feel safe to me, but it was attractive. I glanced over to make sure his ring finger did not have a ring on it and continued on with our conversation.

Joel described his sister and brother-in-law and their adoption process and the excitement of his three nieces as they welcomed their new little brother. He told me each of their names and how his sister and brother-in-law chose the name for their newly adopted son. Getting a glimpse of Joel's character was stunning. All I knew was this man's first name, and yet I had an immediate respect for him.

As we lingered at the little Italian restaurant in the middle of Oxford, England, I learned more of Joel's story. He had recently left the United States Air Force and was taking a year to study theology at Oxford University. He was attending the same college at Oxford that I was about to attend and was a classmate of Jason's. I later found out that Jason intentionally invited Joel to join our meal, hoping the two of us would hit it off. We did, and we enjoyed each other's company as we talked late into the evening.

Just one week later, Joel asked Jason's permission to date me. This was important to me, a fatherless girl, and that evening Joel took me to dinner and asked me to be his girlfriend. He was very intentional and so kind. Without knowing my full story, Joel captured my heart quicker than I knew it was available.

We dated for a year after meeting in Oxford and had a short six-month engagement before Jason later married us. A year and a half later, we welcomed our first son. Today I am more in love with this man than the day I married him. Joel is an even better man than I originally thought. He is faithful. He is patient. He is a family man. He has restored my heart in areas I didn't even know were desolate and brittle. He was the opposite of so much I'd experienced. He was steady when I was used to instability. He was consistent when I was used to unpredictability. He was faithful when I was used to abandonment. He was kind when I was used to cruel treatment. God used Joel Allen to give me a new name, and I am grateful for it.

While Joel was not the answer to my problems, my new name—Esther Allen—has brought me deep, unspeakable joy. This former independent, Beyoncé-listening, proud-to-be-single Esther Fleece became Esther Allen—Joel Allen's bride. Embracing my name change was a gradual process, and I think it happened in my heart long before it happened on an actual sheet of paper. The discovery of my new name was less about finding a husband and more about finding out I was loved, known, and desired—even before a ring went on my finger or I received my "MRS degree."

The changing of our names signals that a change has happened in us. This is precisely why God has new names for us and wants us to live out of these new names.

I had a new name and identity even before I met Joel; I just didn't know how to live out of it confidently. My new name and your new name don't come when we get married or when we achieve enough spiritual clout in our walk with God. Our first new name is "Son" or "Daughter" when we're adopted by God and become His child forever. This makes a spiritual name change even more significant than a physical one. If you're a follower of Jesus, you have been adopted into God's family. You have "new" written all over you!

I know now I was given a new name by God long before I changed my name at the Social Security office, but I didn't know how to discover or live into that new name. I don't want that to happen to you. I want you to know your name from God, and I want you to pursue God and ask Him for it.

WE'RE TEMPTED TO LIVE OUT OF OUR OLD NAMES AND LABELS

I wonder why so many of us are tempted to live as if we're identified by our old labels. The word *label* hardly ever shows up in the Bible's original languages, and when it does, it's similar to the word *called*—he or she was "called" something. And I think it's easy for us to call others names or call ourselves names that don't really apply.

Naming is more significant than labeling, perhaps because labeling only speaks to the titles others put on us, while *naming* speaks to our very core. Labels are about what's on the outside. Naming goes so much deeper. Maybe our attention has been on labels because we're not yet convinced that we've been completely reidentified by the One who has named us "Daughters" and "Sons."

Before I fully understood the power inherent in the new name God had given me, I had lost sight of my identity, inheritance, and new name. This hadn't happened in a way that caused me to live in blatant, unrepentant sin, but I did live in a way that showed I didn't think I had much to bring to the table. I didn't know my full value and worth. I had roots in God, but when storms came, I questioned who I was to Him and who God was to me. This even became a struggle as Joel and I planned our wedding, and I felt embarrassed that I didn't have a biological family history I was proud of or any financial benefit to bring to our union.

Losing sight of our new name and settling for what we've always been is just another way the enemy tries to rob us of our joy and distract us from claiming our truest identity. This settling isn't only for those who steal, drink too much, or covet; settling can also be living in a way that doesn't align with who God says we are. When we as Christians don't live out of our new name, we are usually agreeing with a false label that the enemy has assigned to us. How many of us walk around thinking we are "not being used by God" or "overlooked" or "not worthy" when God has said the opposite!

When we do not align with our new name and identity in Christ, we miss out on spiritual blessings we would receive as a son or daughter in Christ. Most days, I didn't even know God had a new name for me! Not only was my failure to embrace my new name unintentionally separating me from the love of God, but it was keeping me at arm's length from others as well. Whenever I slipped and gave voice to my old name—that of "Orphan"—I was forgetting the names of the people God put around me as family. When I would agree with "fat" or "unattractive," I was accepting the enemy's lie. When we have old names and labels in our vocabulary, we are tempted to live out of them, which dramatically affects how we see ourselves, others, and God.

This is why it's so important for you to realize that you've *already* been renamed by God and that this new reality transforms your identity. This isn't a name for varsity-level Christians (there is no such thing). This new name is for all of us, and God wants us to move past our old labels to be identified by the new name He gives us.

HONORING OTHERS'
TRUE IDENTITIES

Just as we're learning to live into the truth of our new names, our truest identities, we're also called to be people who speak truth to others about who they really are. I think this is why Jesus warns against calling anyone "Raca" or "fool" (Matthew 5:22). We deny the truth of someone's identity as beloved by God when we identify them by a label that denies what is most real and true about them.

A label is a name you are called or a category you place yourself in. A new name is given when God does something inside you.

What new thing has God done inside you, and are you living out of the new name He has given you—this name that is different from your old label or circumstance? Your new name will make you different and cause you to live and believe differently. How are you experiencing this newness, this *kainos*, where you are "not found exactly like this before"?

It's tempting to reduce others by identifying them by their labels. I hear it when women use ugly words to describe other women as "too assertive," "controlling," or "gossips." I notice it when Democrats and Republicans give one another unfair labels that diminish the fullness of who they really are. We do it when we label a precious and complex human being as "too emotional" or "a piece of work" or "unstable." We are not our old labels, and when we assign others to one of these reductionist categories, we miss out on the opportunity to really know them and to affirm who they are in God.

And guess what? One of the clues we're given to discover who others really are and who we really are is found in God's own names. The identity He proclaims over us has been there from the beginning, and it is the invitation of a lifetime to discover the name, identity, and inheritance He has given us.

YOUR NEW NAME MATTERS TO GOD

The birth name chosen for me didn't have much significance for most of my life. But today that name has infinite meaning.

Esther means "star," and I want to shine for God.

Esther in the Bible was an orphan, but she was used by God. In a similar way, although I was abandoned by my biological family, I too want to be used by God.

Queen Esther was courageous, and remembering her name and legacy gives me courage when I want to be timid about my faith or shy about my calling. Knowing that our names have meaning can give us a boldness and confidence to live for God in a world that thinks we are foolish.

Not only is God redeeming my earthly name, but He has exchanged my old name, "Abandoned," for the new names— "Beloved," "Chosen," "Loved," "Adopted," and "Daughter." And just as Christ gave meaning to my past, present, and future, He does the same for you. He redeems your old name, and He is at work even now to communicate to you your new name.

The last book in the New Testament announces that we are given a new name when we overcome, when we are victorious (Revelation 2:17). The sense here is of "carrying off the victory." I wrote this book because I want you to carry off the victory. I want you to know your new name, and I want you to walk it out. I want you to finish strong, with your new name intact, not crumbling under the pressures and stresses of the old labels we've all too often settled for. You have infinite value to God, and no matter what your past is or what former label or name was given to you, God has a new name waiting that is unique to you.

A new chapter with your new name is waiting to be written. We see lessons of character in biblical name-changing that go beyond just trusting God, and we'll examine them throughout this book. The biblical characters received name changes in unique ways. No two name changes were alike! This shows us the creativity of God's name-changing process. It shows how deeply intimate and personal the God of the universe is. If He names the stars and knows the number of hairs on our heads, surely He has a life-giving new name for each of us.

What is God doing inside you right now? Scripture is full of examples of people who were taught by the experiences God took them through. God can use all sorts of circumstances to teach us. God works through His Word, through people, and through our circumstances. Many times our new names are right in front of us. Are you grabbing hold of your new name and living out of it?

The Bible shows us again and again how our God is the God of new things. God does new things in the world (Isaiah 42:9; 43:19). God's mercies to us are new every morning (Lamentations 3:22), and He puts a new song in our mouths (Psalm 40:3). God gives us a new heart (Ezekiel 36:26) and puts a new spirit in us (Ezekiel 11:19).

Knowing our new name helps us live into a new reality. No matter what season of life we find ourselves in, God is constantly putting us in a position to be made new. And the newness God does inside us puts Him on display to the world around us.

For Further Reflection

Reflection: Do you know the meaning of your earthly name? If not, look it up. What have you been called or labeled? What labels have hurt you?

Prayer of Faith: Father God, if all the miracles in the Bible were in Your name and because of Your name, clearly Your name is important. Help me to learn that Your name matters and honor You appropriately. Help me to hear from You what my new name is. Give me faith to believe that You have a new name and identity for me. Thank You that I don't have to live out of my old name or label, but I can see and celebrate the new thing You are doing inside me. Help me to hear You and believe what You say. I pray all these things in the *name* of Jesus. Amen.

Verses to Believe: Matthew 17:20; Luke 17:6; 2 Corinthians 5:17

Labels That Limit

Circle which of the old labels you have believed about yourself.

Abandoned	Forgotten
Chained to Past	Gossip
Disabled	Homeless
Don't Belong	Ignored
Dropout	Introverted
Emotional	Loser
Fat	Mistreated
Fatherless	No Good

Not Engaging

Not Used by God

Orphan

Overlooked

Overweight

Piece of Work

Poor

Raca/Fool

Rebel

Rejected

Sufferer

Too Assertive/Controlling

Too Shy/Introverted

Treated Cruelly

Ugly

Unattractive

Undesirable

Unemployed

Unseen

Unsettled

Unstable

Unworthy

Victim

Your New Name

Circle which of the new names you want to live out of.

Adopted

Beauty

Beloved Daughter/Son/
   Child of God

Bride

Called

Chosen

Christian

Clean

Consistent

Faithful

Fisher of People

Follower of the Way

Free Indeed

Fresh

Individual/Distinct/Unique

Kind

Loved

Minister of the New Covenant

New

New Creation

Overcomer

Pleasing to God

Seen and Heard

Set Apart

Steady

CHAPTER 2

How You Can Incorrectly Name Yourself

"See, I am doing a new thing!
Now it springs up; do you not perceive it?
I am making a way in the wilderness
and streams in the wasteland."

ISAIAH 43:19

It was the best vacation of my entire life. Under sunny skies and a warm breeze, Joel and I dipped our toes in the sand on our honeymoon. I had never felt so loved. Our quick engagement and wedding planning season had left me exhausted, and we were ready for this much-needed break. My heart felt ignited in a way I never knew was humanly possible. For the first time in my life, I felt alive, chosen, and deeply loved.

After a quick lunch on the beach, we headed to our room to change into tennis shoes and go for a walk. Joel and I love going for walks together—from the cobblestone streets of Oxford to the beaches of Mexico. We grabbed our phones to take a selfie before we left, and up popped a message from a biological family member I hadn't spoken to in twenty years.

My heart sank as I wished I had kept my phone off, and Joel noticed the change in my demeanor instantly.

"What's wrong?" he asked me.

I felt anxious and had a hard time finding the words to describe my heart, which now felt shattered. How could just seeing the name of someone who had wounded me significantly continue to have a negative effect all these years later?

There is power in a name.

I hadn't been in a relationship with my biological family in decades, although for the previous three years, my father had been stalking me at my workplace and home. He suffered from mental illnesses that led him to behave neurotically. For years I was the target of his instability, and I lived in fear of him. I lived most of my life looking over my shoulder and having to be very careful about my whereabouts. I didn't even tell people where we were going on our honeymoon, just to be safe. But now, after marrying Joel, for the first time in years I felt I could breathe again.

With Joel by my side, I listened to the voice mail that shared the news that my biological father had died. It gave me a gut-wrenching feeling of grief and, oddly, relief. Even an abandoned child cries when their absent parent dies.

I was heartbroken and confused, and I couldn't imagine why at the happiest time of my life, I would receive such news. It's like one minute we know ourselves to be loved like God says we are, and the next minute the enemy is tapping us on the shoulder or slapping us in the face, reminding us of the old labels that no longer define us.

In one phone call, I forgot my honeymoon bliss and was left to pick up broken pieces once again. Life felt unfair, and God seemed unkind. Would I ever be able to live out of my new names and new identity, or would this brokenness and sadness follow me the rest of my days?

After our honeymoon, we headed to Michigan where the families who took me in during high school were putting on a wedding reception for us. It was a meaningful visit, especially because I could introduce Joel to so many important people in my life. After our scheduled celebration, we were going to visit the church where I grew up and meet with my former pastor.

I arrived at Kensington Church and was escorted to the bridal suite—the newest and prettiest room in the church. Pastor Dave and I were going to record a video to share my story with the church. He was one of the first to read and support my first book. It felt like a fatherly blessing even as I was grieving the loss of my earthly dad. That fact wasn't lost on me, as I was a new bride returning from her honeymoon happy and in love, just as much as I was an abandoned and now grieving daughter. Real life hits hard sometimes. I wanted to walk into this bridal suite confidently with my new name intact, but instead I was struggling with old names and labels I used to be known by.

I wanted so badly to talk about my excitement for the book and my marriage, and about my happiness at seeing everyone again. All of these things were true. And yet earlier that morning, I was picking out a Scripture verse for my biological father's grave. The father who left me as a child. The father who haunted me for years. The father who wasn't present for my celebrations or my graduations—and wasn't even invited to my wedding. My eyes were puffy, and I knew that no amount of makeup could cover the pain. I was in a safe place, but these old labels of "unwanted" and "unloved" still haunted me. I was simultaneously happy and hurting. I wondered if I would ever be a woman who was having just an average, uneventful day.

Have you ever been labeled "the cheerful one"? Or perhaps you have the reputation of always being upbeat and positive? That kind of reputation makes it hard for people like us to have a bad day. Yet I was having a very bad day.

There are new names for all of us who trust God and have been adopted into His family. But first we have to let go of the labels that have kept us from our true identity. Let's take a look at some of these labels to identify which ones have stuck with us and held us back.

LABELS THAT LIMIT

We all face difficult things in life, and sometimes it isn't always what happened to us that affects us so deeply, but what we believe about ourselves as a result. When I was orphaned, I came to believe I was unlovable. When no guys pursued me to be their girlfriend in high school or college, I came to believe I was undesirable. What was the entry point for your false name or label? Identifying what we are *not* will help us hear who we *are*.

You Are Not Your Past

My greatest challenge after hearing of my father's death was to refrain from replaying my *orphanness* again and again. The enemy wanted to rob me of my present chosenness by reminding me of my former orphanness. I had just been chosen by Joel to be his wife, yet the enemy was wanting me to dredge up old wounds that had already been healed. We are not named by our past. Our past sins do not define us, nor do things that were done to us define us. These things in our past do not dictate or determine our destiny.

For years when I tried to live a pure life in middle school and high school, I was labeled a "prude" by a lot of guys I went to school with. I distinctly remember social gatherings where I felt left out and undesirable because of my conviction to not show physical affection to someone other than my husband. After making it through those years, I was labeled "marriage material" by my group of guy friends in college. These guys were fun and probably meant well, but labeling me "marriage material" meant I certainly wasn't datable.

I have friends who despise the label "teen mom" or "pregnant out of wedlock." It hurts anytime we are labeled by our actions, as if they are the whole of who we are. The enemy will lie to us, no matter our past, and try to use our sin or our strong convictions to label us and prevent us from seeing ourselves for who God says we really are.

Christian author and speaker Christine Caine says we need to make who God is and what He's done for us bigger than what has been done to us.[2] This doesn't mean we ignore what has been done to us; rather, we identify what was done to us and the labels we gave ourselves as a result.

If you grew up in poverty, you are more than a "poor person." If you experienced homelessness for a period of time, you are more than a "homeless person." "Poor" or "homeless" may be a descriptor or association, but it is not a status or identity. The enemy will do everything he can to keep us in our past. It's one of the reasons I don't like the term "foster children." There are children in foster care, but there are no "foster children." A child's name and identity are not the unfortunate circumstances they find themselves in.

Our past serves a purpose, and we need to do the hard work to heal and move on in healthy ways. Ignoring our past or ignoring our old names will provide a healing that takes place in name only—one that won't benefit our spiritual walk or anyone who walks alongside us. Many times God will remind us of the painful feelings and emotions from our past so we'll seek healing for them.

I used to be confused when God would bring a painful memory to mind. I didn't know what to do with it. And sometimes I even gave the enemy credit—"The devil is reminding me of painful things"—when he did not deserve the credit. Sometimes God brings to mind painful things so we'll talk to Him about it. If you were labeled as "too loud," "too quiet," or "alone," God wants you to talk to Him about it.

When we ground our identity in the past, we put limits on our future. What if we put emphasis on our new names and what God has done inside us instead of highlighting the names of our past? What if we make God's name known by putting our emphasis on Him and living out of our new names? Old labels are not who we are, and we don't have to hold on to them.

YOU ARE NOT YOUR CIRCUMSTANCES

This truth can be challenging for those of us who face difficult circumstances. If you're unemployed or going through a rough breakup or looking for love that seems nowhere to be found, it's all too easy to take your relationship or employment status personally. You are so much more than your relationship status or your job! When we use qualifiers as our names, we make little progress in knowing our true names.

A few months before our wedding, our dear friend Nabeel Qureshi was diagnosed with stage 4 stomach cancer. As his cancer took a turn for the worse, we couldn't fathom why our good friend would have cancer before his thirtieth birthday. He had so much life yet to live, with a wife and young daughter at home. We prayed daily for Nabeel's healing. Less than a year later, cancer would end Nabeel's earthly life, and we dropped everything to be present with his wife and attend the funeral.

Nabeel and his wife, Michelle, were two of the first friends Joel and I met in Oxford. The Qureshis allowed me to stay in their home during my summer study program and quickly introduced me to many other friends in Oxford. Nabeel was the sort of person who never met a stranger, and their home was constantly full of hospitality, food, and joy. He had a brilliant mind and was used by God around the world to share in love the differences between Islam and Christianity.

Just days after the funeral, Michelle told me she wasn't going to take on "Widow" as her new name. I was stunned at her ability to say this so quickly after her husband's death. Michelle explained that "widow" is a descriptive term that will occasionally need to be used, but "Widow" was not her new name or identity. Michelle said she was and is Nabeel's wife. She boldly proclaimed that their young daughter, Ayah, will always be Nabeel's daughter, and no circumstance could ever change that. Michelle didn't need to take on the name "Widow" or "Single Mom" based on her circumstances. She was Michelle, and she wanted to be known by her name. And we don't need to let our circumstances rename us either.

It's so easy to mistake descriptive words, statuses, or circumstances as our new names. Your name is not "Widow," "Infertile," "Single Parent," or "Divorced." You don't have to be embarrassed if you're labeled a "young mom" or feel insecure about wrinkles if you're called an "old mom" when you drop off your son or daughter at school. Can you imagine if God chose us or named us based on external qualifiers? I am so glad He sees past these things and looks at our hearts.

The enemy wants to keep us incorrectly named because it keeps our eyes on our circumstances and not on the cross. But we are more than our temporary circumstances. Thank goodness! God will always call us by our names, and our dire (or even delightful) circumstances will never define who we are to God.

Have you ever named yourself based on your circumstance? We're often tempted to overidentify with our circumstances or our status. We can interpret a good day at work to mean we should be the boss. Or we can interpret a bad day in parenting to mean we are a bad parent. Overidentifying with our circumstances prevents us from hearing God's new name for us. We are not our circumstances on either a good day or a bad day, and reminding ourselves of this truth is a discipline we need to live out on a daily basis. Christian author Judy Douglass says, "God always knows which name to call us in every circumstance."[3]

As followers of Christ, our most common name in the Bible is the word *disciple*—a word used more than 250 times in the New Testament. Some of you have believed you're not very smart, or that you deserve to be the last one chosen for a team or for your dream job. But this name says otherwise. This name means you were chosen to follow Christ and represent Him. God is not embarrassed that you are His!

We can default to this name when we're tempted to name ourselves based on our circumstances. We don't belong to God because of what we accomplish or what we can offer Him. God loves us even when we are not producing something for Him. We don't have to be orphans and widows anymore, and when we let go of these labels, we are free to live out of who He says we are. We can call ourselves disciples and know that we belong to God.

You Are Not Your Limitations

Joel's family has been in health care for generations. My in-laws, Brad and Nancy Allen, started a company that provides housing, employment, and health care for adults with intellectual and developmental disabilities. Their clients (who are also their friends) were born with Down syndrome, autism, cerebral palsy, fetal alcohol syndrome, and other disabilities that require them to have additional assistance in life.

Too often we underestimate this group of bright and compassionate people with special abilities who reflect the heart and character of God. One of my favorite days each year is the day of the company Christmas party. As a family, we serve food and spend time with the clients, and this group knows how to party! They are great singers and dancers. They have great imaginations and find joy in seemingly little things. They care for one another. They are not as limited as we may make them out to be.

As I served brunch at the party one year, a client asked me if I knew the gospel. It caught me off guard, as I saw myself as being in a position to help, and she had a similar posture toward me. This young woman told me her name was Kirsten and that she was God's daughter. It gave me such delight to hear someone introduce herself this way! Kirsten told me all about the cross and the resurrection and said she was going to live with God forever one day. She asked me if I was going to live there too.

It struck me that this young woman whom the world names "Disabled" had her name and identity more intact than most of us do. Kirsten knew who she was and whose she was. Her eyes were not fixed on her disability, her circumstances, or her limitations. Kirsten knew whom she belonged to and where her value came from. I was so impacted by Kirsten that I began to reconsider how I introduce myself.

What if we began introducing ourselves as God sees us? Doing so would not be arrogant or prideful; rather, this living out of our new names might provoke others to live out who God says they really are. What if we began sharing what God has named us instead of holding on to the old labels we've settled for?

Look no further than the Bible to learn some of the new names we possess. God's children are called His handiwork (Ephesians 2:10), and this is based on who we are, not on what we do. Kirsten is God's creation, made in God's image. She was God's handiwork before she said or did anything for God. The same goes for her roommate, Della, who is nonverbal and unable to express who she is to God and who He is to her. We are named God's handiwork, His best creation, before we ever produce anything for Him. Isn't that something?

Many of us spend our lives trying to earn God's approval, even though our new names are given to us because of who He is, not because of what we do. Before we were formed in our mothers' wombs, God knew us (Jeremiah 1:5) and had plans and purposes for us. When we focus on our abilities or disabilities, we have a narrow view of God, which in turn limits all we do and see.

When we become new creations in God (2 Corinthians 5:17), the core of who we are changes. We go from being dead to being alive. And this doesn't stop at the moment of our salvation. Our abilities do not define us, nor do our disabilities rename us. As children of God, we are called imitators of God (1 Thessalonians 1:6). We are His instruments (2 Timothy 2:20–21). This is part of our new name and our calling.

You Are Not What Others Call You

Luther Elliss was one of the first men to show me what the love of a safe father looked like. Luther and his wife took me in during my high school years. I met them at my church and began nannying for them when they had five children. This family, of which I'm now a part, has grown to thirteen children, both biologically and through adoption.

Luther had a successful career in professional football as a defensive tackle for the Detroit Lions and the Denver Broncos. He is of Samoan descent, a culture that loves and values family. The Ellisses are the first ones who taught me that family goes beyond bloodlines. Both Luther and Rebecca have a heart for the fatherless, and it's part of the reason they noticed me when I needed a family. The Ellisses have funded both local and global ministries for the cause of the orphan and the fatherless. I know several families in the NFL who have grown their families through adoption, all because of Luther and Rebecca's influence and financial support.

Luther was one of the men from whom Joel asked permission to marry me, and one of four father figures who walked me down the aisle to give me away on my wedding day. Rebecca stood with me as a bridesmaid, and their children—my siblings—were all present in the front of the church. I would do anything for this family that gave everything to me.

While I lived with the Ellisses, I had no idea how much money Luther made in his profession. I only knew they were incredibly generous. I saw people cross boundaries to ask the Ellisses for money and possessions, and this always rubbed me the wrong way. Because I wanted the Ellisses to know I loved them for who they are and not for what they could offer me, I never spoke with them about their money.

I saw Luther and Rebecca consistently give toward helping put food on people's tables. They organized Detroit Lions Thanksgiving food drives and supported the United Way. I saw them take care of mortgage payments for single moms. I remember one Christmas when I saw beautifully wrapped packages of toys piled up in their dining room and found out they stayed up the night before to wrap them for underprivileged children in Detroit. This family gave and gave and gave until nothing was left for themselves.

And while it's true that we can never outgive God, through some unfortunate circumstances, the Ellisses filed for bankruptcy five years after Luther's NFL career ended. I was devastated when this family that had never withheld from me went through setback and loss. In the coming years, I watched the most generous people I know struggle in a way my slim nonprofit salary could not fix. What made it worse were the headlines that gloated over their loss, as if wealthy NFL players somehow deserve criticism.

Luther played college football in Utah, and when a Utah newspaper ran a cover story titled "From Riches to Rags," it showed how quickly friends scatter when life gets tough. I was angry at the disrespect that people showed the Ellisses, like any protective daughter would be. For years I had seen Luther give freely and tirelessly to the people of Utah. He started and funded football camps, served on the board for an adoption agency, and more. How could this newspaper say such unkind things about someone they had praised just a few years before? As I tried to remind Luther and Rebecca that they were not what the headlines said, it was difficult to believe they were not named by what everyone else was calling them.

Have you been called an unkind name? Maybe it wasn't in a headline, but it came from an old friend. Maybe you've been called "a failure" or "lazy," or a teacher said, "You're not smart enough." Perhaps you heard from parents or a coach that you wouldn't amount to much. Maybe you were even called "entitled" by your own parents. No matter what negative thing people have said *about* you, this is not what God's name is *for* you. God sees much deeper than the external cards we've been dealt and looks into our hearts (1 Samuel 16:7). God calls us a new name based on who He sees us as, not on who others say we are. Character matters to God. Our hearts matter to God.

Sixty times in the New Testament, God's children are called saints. This can be translated as "holy people" or, simply put, "set-apart people." This is the third most common name for us in Scripture. Think of that: God calls you a saint!

Think of Mother Teresa, whom many know as a saint. She was rich in all the right things in life. Mother Teresa wasn't a saint because of her material wealth or her business expertise or acumen; she was known by her love. After her death, Mother Teresa was bestowed the honor of sainthood by the Catholic Church, and this had little to do with what others said about her. Rather, it had everything to do with her faithful actions.

I remember a book came out shortly after her death that contained some of her writings. Some harsh criticism emerged in evangelical circles as people found fault with some of her private journal entries. Never mind that many of us go through long periods and seasons of questioning God, and few of us would want someone reading our journals about it. Imagine people wanting to dismiss a lifetime of work, all because Mother Teresa's personal diaries included things that made their faith uncomfortable.

Even saints will have critics. How do we handle criticism over our name when it comes? Do we ignore it, or do we run from it? Do we fight against people, or do we go to God and ask Him what He calls us? It's God's vote that counts, not the votes of many others who will laugh at our names here on earth.

I truly believe Luther and Rebecca Elliss are called saints by God. I recently found out that they took in two more teens in need of a home. God sees their names and character. He sees their checkbook too and doesn't define them by it. God sees how the Ellisses have poured their lives into others and given sacrificially to meet others' needs.

If you are a child of God, you too are called a saint. Surely we can trust this affirmation rather than the untrue and unkind words of gossip, envy, malice, and slander that will be spoken against us. Even Jesus Himself was misunderstood by friends and loved ones.

YOU ARE NOT NAMED BY WHAT YOU DO (OR BY ANY EXTERNAL IDENTIFIER)

Luther Elliss is more than a former National Football League player, and you are more than what you do for a living. So much of our lives involves work. We spend a lot of time at work. I get it. Work is a fact of life, and it pays the bills. Work is important, but it does not name us. I believe God has given us the gift of work, and we are to thank Him for it. But we are not to take our occupations, the daily work we do, and substitute them as our primary names and identities.

My husband, Joel, and I were at the opening of the Museum of the Bible in Washington, D.C.—a museum project started by the Green Family of Hobby Lobby—and we were excited to meet others who helped this project come to fruition. The museum has six floors and 430,000 square feet of history, archaeology, and more as it showcases the Bible and its impact on culture.

As we stepped into a crowded elevator on the way to an

evening event, I recognized the tall man standing next to me from television. I knew he was in the media, but I couldn't come up with the show he was on. Joel, wanting to be friendly, started a casual conversation in which he asked the man what he did and how he had heard about the museum. The man answered, "I work for the president of the United States." Once we exited the elevator, he quickly walked away.

It was clear he took a lot of pride in his job and was a bit annoyed that we didn't recognize him as someone who worked in the current administration. As Joel and I returned to our hotel room that evening, we googled the man, only to find out he had been let go by the president months prior. This man who had recently been removed from a high position of power was still identifying himself with his old career.

Now, I've experienced a staff reduction and job loss, and it's difficult to go through. Many of us will go through a significant job change or job loss in our lives, and that can be hard and scary. Times of job transition can make us feel insecure about who we are and what we have to offer. A friend once said to me that one of the worst names to take on is "Unemployed."

As difficult as unemployment is to navigate, our work status or title is never determinative of who we truly are. When we pair who we are with what we do, we are giving our job our identity rather than God. Don't be like this man who continued to tell people he worked for the president when that season was long gone.

God has new things for us to do and fresh things for us to become in this life. Whether we're working for the president of the United States, clocking in at a coffee shop, or pastoring a local church, our job is not our main title. Some pastors even have a hard time taking a vacation as they give themselves so fully to their work in the church. God doesn't need our performance, and many times our new names are revealed when we least expect it—in seasons of slowness, trials, and rest.

While our work "for the glory of God" should be done to the best of our ability (1 Corinthians 10:31), our ability should not become our identity. We see in the Bible that everyday fishermen became fishers of people. Be open to God giving you a name outside of your career field. We don't need to put limits on God or on ourselves.

Although we're not identified by what we *do*, some of the names God gives us can be expressed in our loving response to God. What we do flows from who we are rather than the other way around.

Scripture calls us Christ's ambassadors (2 Corinthians 5:20). We are ones who go on errands for God (Proverbs 13:17; Isaiah 18:2; Jeremiah 49:14). We are interpreters and messengers for God (2 Chronicles 32:31; 35:21). Most of us have not met with a foreign ambassador, but this doesn't stop God from calling us one of His ambassadors. God qualifies us long before we show up with our résumé.

YOU ARE MORE THAN YOUR STRENGTHS AND ACCOMPLISHMENTS

My friend Sara has impeccable manners. She was an honor student, served in student government, and always looked put together when we were classmates at a Christian university. It was one of the first times in my life I was exposed to moral people who grew up with intact families. I felt like my brokenness stood out sorely next to a pretty, polite, and put-together person like Sara.

Sara's dorm was always pristine, and she had note cards that she'd send to people to encourage them. While I spent late nights in the library studying, trying to maintain a C average, good grades seemed to come easy for Sara. And not only good grades, but cooking, singing, serving others—you name it. If Sara put her hands to it, it turned to gold.

One of the benefits of social media is that it allows us to stay in touch with friends years (okay, decades) after college. Sara reached out to me in complete humility, sharing how even positive labels have undermined her ministry inside the church and caused her to feel left out.

You see, Sara is a pastor's wife who gets labeled "perfect" and told she comes across like Mary Poppins—someone who has it all together. Sara loves her family, and it shows. She chooses to homeschool, makes three meals a day for her family, and keeps a neat and tidy home. Sara struggles with her label of "perfect"; she never intended to come across this way. Sara is kept at arm's length because of her "old-fashioned" outlook on womanhood— her calling as a pastor's wife and stay-at-home mom—and this label (whether or not it's true) has prevented others from getting to know her.

Labels can sometimes be aimed at the good and positive things we all strive for in life. Maybe you've been called "too nice" or have been avoided because of your wealth. My friend Emily feels wounded for being called "normal" in elementary school, when all she wanted to do was stand out, make a difference, and live passionately. No matter what side of the spectrum we fall on, even positive names, associations, and labels have the potential to leave us feeling isolated and alone.

You are not "just a mom"—God loves the role and title of mother. But just as you choose a name for your children because you see a bright future for them, God sees a bright future for you too. Your calling as a mom is not your sole identifier as a woman of God.

If I were to describe Sara, I would say she is bright, compassionate, lovely, humble, servant-hearted, faithful, loyal, and more. We would look for all of these qualities in a friendship. Why, then, is it hard for Sara to break in? Why are Sara's strengths, like her spirituality and depth of character, used against her? It's because labels can lie, limit, and give us an easy out from getting to know someone at a deeper level. Have you been called "too smart" or "too pretty" or maybe even "normal" when you wanted to be unique?

We are not our successes, our highlight reels, or our financial contributions. We are more than our best days, our good grades, and our lucrative business deals. Sara desires to break past these labels and have healthy relationships with people. I bet you do too. Have your strengths ever caused you to feel unpursued and unknown?

Labels limit our potential relationships and prevent us from working together as the body of Christ to accomplish God's will on earth. But God thinks higher than labels that limit. All of us want to be given the opportunity to be known beyond the group we're a part of. Let's not keep ourselves or others at arm's length because of a strength, a success, or a "guilt by association" philosophical or theological camp. Let's look deeper than the label and get to know people by their real names.

WHAT LABEL WRONGLY DEFINES YOU?

What about you? Can you think of ways you've incorrectly named yourself? Have you named yourself based on what has been done to you? Maybe you see the wrong done to you and focus on that part of your past rather than on the new name that God wants to bestow as a part of your healing. Do you struggle to see yourself beyond what you've been called in the past or beyond your past decisions?

Perhaps there's a name or circumstance not described above that fits you. Perhaps you don't believe you are worthy, or you avoid close relationships out of insecurity, or your perfectionism is leaving you paralyzed. We all get our names wrong. Having the awareness of our false names and labels will help us identify what we are not. And when we know what we are not, we prepare our hearts to hear who we really are.

If you are a follower of Christ, you are a child of God. If God has made you new, you are a saint. You are a new creation, and there are more new names that God has waiting for you. We do not earn our new names; they are benefits given to us as children of God.

In addition to being ambassadors, we are farmers (2 Timothy 2:6) and fishers of people (Mark 1:17). These names are just as important to God as our regular occupations, maybe even more so, because they speak of our new identity in Christ.

No matter what our occupation, are we living as ministers of the new covenant (2 Corinthians 3:6)? We are *all* ministers, not just those of us with degrees. We, the children of God, are all spokespeople for God. Our occupations do not take away from or add to our names and job descriptions as followers of Christ. Do we take more pride in the job we think we earned or in the new name we've been given by God Himself?

Just as most of us don't see the hard work of a farmer that allows us to have food on our tables, most of us will not see the intimate, personal work God does inside us. What the world will see, however, is how we live out of our new names. Are we living loved? Do we live like we are God's kids? Do others see our saintliness and consider us blessed? Our inner transformation will display itself outwardly through our new name. But in order to hear our new name, we must be willing to throw off old names and labels that don't belong to us.

BROTHERS AND SISTERS

Throughout his first letter to the Thessalonians, Paul affirmed the believers for their brotherly love for one another, which was a marker of someone who had faith. In my moment of great distress when my biological family abandoned me, the church, my spiritual family, showed me love. When my earthly father passed away, my husband was present for me as physical family around me. Sometimes we have to look around us to see how God is providing instead of dwelling on what the enemy is stealing. I wonder if we recognize that God's people are present in our times of need to remind us that God is with us.

The phrase "brothers and sisters" is used in Scripture to describe Christians—referring to both men and women (Galatians 3:28) who have been born again and have become children of God (John 1:12). We are all creations of God made in His image, but not all of us are God's children. God wants us all to be His children, but just because we are alive and breathing does not make us His children. Those of you who are parents will understand this. Just because you're a parent of one, two, or three children doesn't mean you are the parent of every child in your child's class. When we accept Christ as our personal Savior, we are given a new name, a new identity, and a new family. This is when we are given our first new name—"Child of God" (1 John 3:1).

Most of us struggle with our new name and identity. We will typically face internal struggles before we face external difficulties. We will wrestle with our purpose and our identity before we face a challenge in our work or personal life. We may face anxiety when trying something new or feel inadequate to tackle a new endeavor. But if we take time to know who we are in Christ—and not just know our new names in our minds but meditate on them and let them dwell in our hearts—the external pressures and challenges we face will not sever our faith.

If in your inmost parts you feel something is wrong with you or you are paralyzed by people pleasing, living out of the new name God has for you will be extremely difficult. But hearing our new name from God changes things. A name change follows a heart and mind-set change. When we know who we are, confidence builds and identity gets rooted and more firmly established. Knowing our new name internally will be the tool that helps us take an external stand for our faith when other names get thrown at us.

Even with my new name of Esther Allen, as a child of God and a new bride, I needed support to live out of my new name. I needed friends and family to recognize my new identity and help me continue to live into it. And even when given my new name, I still felt deeply broken and too familiar with my old labels. Because of Christ's family, I did not need to process my new name alone. And you don't need to either. If you are a Christian, you're not alone. The enemy may want you to feel broken or "too dull" to process deep things, but the family of God is a gift to all of us to help process our new names. New names and identities are given to us by God, but that doesn't mean we always see them right away or even know how to live out of our new God-given identity.

Knowing our new name is a key in our ability to overcome the difficult things life brings our way. Living out of our new name will take time. Not being defined by our circumstances will take time. We may need those around us to help us identify the wrong names and labels we are living out of. Knowing what God says about us and treasuring this name and identity in our heart before the storms come will help us overcome.

Who around you can help you process your new name? Perhaps there is a mentor or teacher who can walk with you and encourage you with the true things God says about you. Maybe there is a pastor or friend who can help you live out of this new identity. We are not given a new name and expected to live out of this new name alone.

As my names were changing, God provided a spouse and allowed me to reconnect with the pastor of my youth. We all need trusted loved ones to remind us of who we are. In the journey of living out our new name, we all benefit from surrounding ourselves with truth-tellers. Even Jesus Himself had people to process life with. Let's begin by taking a look at old names and labels we've wrongly associated with. As you find yourself identifying with any of these, think of those around you who can encourage you on your "new name" journey.

THE LITTLE THINGS THAT HOLD US BACK

Establishing a familiarity with our new name will not be a quick fix, nor will it be an overnight path to break unhealthy cycles of dysfunction. Those of us with a past (hint: all of us) will need to spend intentional moments ensuring that our past brokenness does not become our present or future brokenness. Our hope here lies in Christ and in the same power that raised Him from the dead (Romans 8:11), empowering us to live in a different way than those who have gone before us.

When we are in Christ Jesus, we have a new identity and a new inheritance. However, we will still have to intentionally pursue wholeness, healing, and new patterns of thinking and behavior. And yes, some of us will have to work harder for wholeness and healing than others because of the cards we've been dealt. This is not God's fault, nor does it indicate God's neglect of you. This is a result of living in a fallen world and of the reality that every human being we associate with has a sinful nature.

We all know we should stay away from sin, but there is a synonym for sin in Scripture that is often left out of our Christian vocabulary—*iniquity*. I want us to be aware of our iniquity because I think it's one of the main reasons we don't live out of our new names. *Iniquity* refers to "crookedness" and "perverseness." The reason we need to pay attention to iniquity is that it is a subtler sin than the things we easily refer to as sin. Because it is a bent toward sin, iniquity is not so easy to recognize. Iniquity can be our bent toward anger and rage or our subtle arrogance.

Sometimes our iniquity is easier for others to see than for us to see in ourselves. We can even make our iniquity sound Christian and give off a sense of false humility. Iniquity can lead us to all kinds of unsafe places, like self-pity or pride. Iniquity can even show up in our attitudes, like when I want designer clothes and look down on those who don't have them.

In a similar way, we can live out of iniquity when we're lazy in prioritizing who God says we are. Some of us wrongly believe that God does not take seriously the lies we believe about ourselves. Iniquity is not a "lesser" sin; it is an inner act of willfulness against God that is contrary to God's character. It makes God out to be a liar, and God cannot lie (Titus 1:2). Iniquity can show up when I believe I am unworthy of God's love and thus avoid approaching Him as a loving Father. Or my iniquity can look like not asking God what He says about me because I'm afraid He will have unkind things to say.

We are prone to iniquity when we believe our own thoughts and feelings above what the Word of God says about us. For example, when I go through a difficult time, my iniquity "bent" is to believe that God does not love me or that God has abandoned me. And while these thoughts may seem harmless, they are not. They are sin against God. What do you bend toward believing about yourself? What does your iniquity bend you toward? Anxiety? Criticism? Entitlement? Depression?

It is important to be aware of our iniquities, because it's so easy to justify them. And when we justify these "bents," at least in our own minds, we continue to live the same way. We are not motivated to change. Iniquities are not "lesser" offenses to God; on the contrary, they are often the start of something very serious. Our bent toward sin can be just as harmful to us as other blatant sins that call for church discipline. Our iniquities need to be acknowledged and repented of just as much as if we were to curse God outright.

> Then I acknowledged my sin to you
>> and did not cover up my iniquity.
> I said, "I will confess
>> my transgressions to the Lord."
> And you forgave
>> the guilt of my sin.
>
> PSALM 32:5

Are we mindful of our iniquities, these "little" areas that can devastatingly prevent us from knowing our new names? When I believed I was not worth loving, I was making God's love out to be a lie. I was believing my iniquity, my bent toward sin, to be more truthful than God Himself. Our iniquities compete with who God says we are, so we not only need to identify our iniquities but must confess them and repent of having believed them—even when we've believed them subconsciously.

Do you believe you've messed up too badly for God to extend His everlasting kindness toward you? Not so. God would delight to give you a new name, season, and story. Do you believe you've lived a certain way for so long that it's too late to learn a new way of thinking, living, or eating? Not so. God has the power to help you overcome. And just because you were something doesn't mean you have to stay that way.

We must keep watch for the enemy, who will try hard to sidetrack us with seemingly little things that become big things and with patterns of thinking that lead us away from God.

For Further Reflection

Reflection: Are there any wrong names or labels you've been holding on to? What do you bend toward believing about yourself? What name have you wrongly called yourself in the past? Who can help identify who you are?

Prayer of Petition: Maker of heaven and earth, if You have names for the stars, how much more do You have a name for me! Help me lift my eyes to You. I want to hear the name You have for me. Please remove any distractions that hinder me from hearing the new name You have for me. Increase my faith, help me overcome my unbelief, and name me! In Jesus' name. Amen.

Verses to Believe: Mark 9:23–25; Luke 17:5

Labels That Limit
Circle which of the old labels you have believed about yourself.

Abandoned	Damaged Goods
Alone	Dead
Angry/Full of Rage	Disabled
Anxious	Divorced
Arrogant/Prideful	Entitled
Avoid Relationships	Failure
Bad Mom/Young Mom/	Fatherless
Old Mom	Foster Child
Bankrupt	Homeless Person
Boring/Dull	Inadequate
Broken	Infertile
Complicated	Insecure

Just a Mom	Separated
Last to Be Chosen	Single Parent
Lazy	Teen Mom
Misfit	Too Broken
Nonverbal	Too Loud
Not Dateable	Too Perfect/Too Nice/Too Pretty
Not Smart Enough	Too Quiet
Not Worth the Time	Too Smart
Orphan	Undesirable
Paralyzed	Unemployed
People Pleaser	Unlovable
Perfectionist	Unloved
Poor Person	Unwanted
Pregnant Out of Wedlock	Unworthy
Prude	Widow
Self-Pitying	Won't Amount to Much

Your New Name

Circle which of the new names you want to live out of.

Alive	God's Daughter/Child/Kid
Blessed	God's Handiwork
Bride	God's Instrument
Brother/Sister	Imitator of God
Chosen	Interpreter for God
Christ's Ambassador	Loved
Confident	Made in God's Image/
Disciple	God's Image Bearer
Errand Runner for God	Messenger for God
Farmer	Minister of the New Covenant
Firmly Established	New Creation
Fisher of People	Saint/Holy/Set Apart
Follower of Christ	Spokesperson
God's Creation	Wife/Husband

CHAPTER 3

Discovering Your New Names

*"I will give them an everlasting name
that will endure forever."*
ISAIAH 56:5

My high school years were turbulent. I was a teenage girl with a mother who didn't care to have me around. My mother would frequently change the locks in our house, forcing me to find a place to sleep and leaving me to fend for myself. I would spend the night on my neighbor's basement couch, stay with a coach, or share a bed with my best friend who didn't want me to sleep on the floor. Each time I found myself kicked out, there was a warm home or family to provide what I needed in that exact moment.

I was usually out of my home for a few weeks—sometimes months—before I returned home. I don't know why I always wanted to return home, other than the fact that it was home, even in all of its dysfunction. Even unhealthy homes have a sense of familiarity to them.

I was a good kid, got good grades, and worked to make ends

meet. I had a few jobs and was always involved in activities at school and at church. My mother wouldn't allow me to get my driver's license, so I depended on rides from others, including complete strangers at times.

Like many teens, I'm sure I was annoying at times. Trying to figure out who I was in an unstable home, I was talkative and strong-willed. But for the vast majority of the time, I was a good girl, doing my best to make it in a home environment where I wasn't known or loved.

On one of the nights I was kicked out of my house, I found myself at church for a Wednesday night service. For the life of me, I can't remember how I got to church that night, but I was so thankful to be there. Church provided relief to my soul and community when I was abandoned. I craved these meetings and always looked forward to going.

Following the hour-long worship service, I found myself in the lobby, wandering aimlessly and wondering how I'd get home. Even in church, people can come and go so quickly that they miss the needs of people right in front of them. Deep in my heart, I knew some of these people would drive me home. We were at church, where we're taught to love our neighbors and to serve others. But my fears and my desire to not be a burden to anyone were stronger than any assurance I might have felt about asking. Worried and sad, I wondered and prayed.

As I wandered in the lobby, I was welcomed by a familiar couple, Luther and Rebecca Elliss. They were the family that gave to others extravagantly. Everyone in church knew the Ellisses. They had a ton of kids and poured so much into the church through their hearts of service.

Luther and Rebecca approached me with their typical, upbeat "Hello, Esther!" but this time was different. Rebecca asked me if I was okay, and Luther asked me if I needed anything. Did I look so disheartened that they knew something bad was going on? I was *not* okay, and I *did* need things, but how do you answer these questions briefly in a church lobby? I became quiet and defensive.

The Ellisses didn't back down or walk away.

"What's going on?" Rebecca asked.

"What do you need?" asked Luther.

They had no way of knowing what I had just gone through. Just hours before, my mother tricked me by asking me to get something out of her car for her, and while I was outside, she closed the door and locked me out. I had no way back in, wasn't even wearing shoes, and knew my worst nightmare had just happened yet again. It was always embarrassing to get kicked out, but this time was one of the worst, as I had no shoes on to pretend I was fine.

I walked barefoot to my teacher's house. She had told me where she lived when she heard about the fights between my mom and me. She said if I ever needed anything to come over, and I felt she meant it. So I showed up at her house with burning feet and borrowed a pair of shoes and called a friend.

My classmate Cindy Meyerand came to pick me up. I was always afraid of being a burden to anyone, so I tried to never overstay my welcome. Cindy picked me up and took me to her home, where I ate dinner with her family. I remember her dad being just as confused as I was as to why and how I was sitting at their dinner table. *How do you make small talk when your life is falling apart? How did I end up homeless again? What will my next move be?*

It must have been the Meyerands who took me to church that night. I stood silently in the lobby, wondering how I would answer the Ellisses' questions.

Without skipping a beat, Luther said, "Esther, we don't know what it is about you, but we feel like you're our daughter. Do you need a place to stay? Do you need a job? Would you like to be our nanny?"

Rebecca followed up on Luther's remarks by asking me to

come over for dinner the following evening and to consider moving in to help them with their five children.

Within minutes, I went from homeless to provided for. Within hours of being kicked out by my birth mother, I was called "Daughter" by a family I hardly knew. Was God speaking to me through the Elliss family? Was God providing for me through these two families—the Meyerands and the Ellisses?

I was orphaned, but overnight I became a nanny to five wonderful children. The Ellisses grew their family each year I lived with them, and in a short period of time, I went from being a nanny to being an older sister. I felt adopted and safe in this home, and the Elliss and Meyerand families not only helped me finish my high school years, but remain in my life to this day.

As believers, we are given new names throughout Scripture. We can too easily overlook these new names, since we're often familiar with just our physical names. Yet our spiritual names are accessible and available to all of us who are in Christ.

WHO GOD SAYS WE ARE

The name "Christian" appears three times in the New Testament—not as many times as I would have thought. We take on Christ's name and become little Christs when we begin to follow Him. The early believers were called Christians because their behavior and speech were like those of Jesus.

> The disciples were called Christians first at Antioch.
> ACTS 11:26

> Then Agrippa said to Paul, "Do you think that in such a short time you can persuade me to be a Christian?"
> ACTS 26:28

However, if you suffer as a Christian, do not be ashamed, but praise God that you bear that name.

1 PETER 4:16

Another common name given to believers was "followers of the Way." Jesus called Himself "the way and the truth and the life" in John 14:6, and followers of Christ labeled themselves as "the Way" in the book of Acts: "However, I admit that I worship the God of our ancestors as a follower of the Way" (Acts 24:14; see 9:2).

Just as I was welcomed into the Elliss and Meyerand families, we are grafted into the family of God. When we are adopted, we not only have a new *home* and belong, but God takes it a step further and gives a whole new *identity*. These names are available to all of us who place our faith in Christ Jesus as our Leader and Lord.

Let's take a look at who God says we are, which is the first step in getting to know our new name.

YOU ARE NAMED "SON" OR "DAUGHTER"

We become sons and daughters of God through our faith and not our deeds: "So in Christ Jesus you are all children of God through faith" (Galatians 3:26).

This was hard for me to grasp, since I was kicked out of my home even when I was acting right. How could God call us His children even when we didn't look like it or behave like it?

It has always bothered me when people say, "Blood is thicker than water," because it is not so with Christ. In Christ, we are adopted into His family, and He does not treat us differently if we are Jew or Gentile. In baptism, we are raised to new life (Colossians 2:12) and show the world who our new Father is (Ephesians 4:4–6). The water of the Spirit, then, is thicker than blood, and Jesus confirms our new family by saying, "Whoever does the will of my Father in heaven is my brother and sister and mother" (Matthew 12:50). For new believers, Spirit is thicker than blood!

It's a common misconception to think we become children of God through good deeds. To become a son or daughter of God, we simply receive the free gift of salvation offered through Jesus. I lived in the Ellisses' large home, and as a high school student, there was no way I was able to afford rent. Paying them back with my babysitting money, compared to Luther's NFL salary, would have been laughable. I could have nannied for the rest of my life and still not come close to making a dent in what I owed them.

So it is with God. We cannot pay Him enough to match the price He has paid for us. We don't pay Him to become His followers, and our good deeds do not keep us in the family of God. We receive Him by faith and are given the right to become His children (John 1:12). I needed to receive the Ellisses' invitation to nanny and live with them, just as we receive God's free gift of salvation by way of Jesus' death on the cross for the forgiveness of our sins. The second we try to pay it back, we're forgetting we are the recipients of a beautiful gift.

After we become a Christian, God begins calling us His child. It was healing for me to hear the word *daughter* come out of Luther's mouth. That name has brought me comfort each day since. And my heart warms when I hear Mom Meyerand speak proudly about me as her daughter when she is with her friends. Do you know that God talks nice about you? He likes you and is glad you are His child.

Even more than a physical daughter, I am a spiritual daughter of God. We need this new name not only in our younger years, but also as we age. Losing a parent by abandonment is hard, but so is losing a parent to death. It can be difficult to hold on to our name "Son" or "Daughter" when we begin to care for our aging parents. There is comfort that we are a son or daughter spiritually even when the name changes or loses meaning on earth.

Pastor Louie Giglio says that the heavenly Father is not a perfected version of our earthly parents; He is the *perfect* Father.[4]

In other words, God is not a better version of your good parent or your not-so-good parent. God is perfectly good, perfectly whole, and perfectly loving, and when we become His children, we receive a perfect Father.

Because we are God's children, God says He will father us: "I will be a Father to you, and you will be my sons and daughters, says the Lord Almighty" (2 Corinthians 6:18). Not only does God call us His children, but we gain permission to call Him by one of His names—Father: "Because you are sons, God has sent the Spirit of his Son into our hearts, crying, 'Abba! Father!'" (Galatians 4:6 ESV).

Luther Elliss went from NFL figure to father figure to me, and I went from a volunteer at the church to adopted daughter in his heart. It would have been tempting to believe I was "undeserving" or "damaged" or to stay insecure, but there came a point when I needed to believe I was a daughter—provided for and loved.

I don't know about you, but learning how to be a good daughter could take up all of my days. Being a daughter did not come naturally to me. I do not naturally rest in God's presence. I would rather perform. I do not naturally talk to God about my day— the good and the bad—but I've learned that this Father-daughter relationship takes time to get used to. God wants us to take time to live out of our new name—"Son" or "Daughter."

Although the enemy hisses to our hearts that we are slaves, Galatians 4:7 confirms, "Therefore you are no longer a slave, but a son; and if a son, then an heir through God" (NASB). Are you a slave, or are you a son or daughter of God? Ask the Spirit to confirm it to you (Romans 8:14). Are you living like a slave or like a child of God? Do you experience joy in knowing who you are to God?

YOU ARE NAMED "ADOPTED CHILD"

The Ellisses added to their family through adoption and more biological children. I got a front-row seat to the beauty and challenges surrounding adoption. They treated all of their children fairly and equally. To this day, there is no distinction between who is adopted and who is biological. The Ellisses are a wonderful example of the family of God. Their children are Native American, Hispanic, African American, Caucasian, Samoan, and more.

As Gentiles, to become Christ followers and take on His name means we are adopted, and "Adopted Child" becomes one of our new names: "He predestined us for adoption to sonship through Jesus Christ, in accordance with his pleasure and will" (Ephesians 1:5).

Just as it was Luther and Rebecca Elliss's pleasure to grow their family by adoption, it is God's pleasure and will to adopt you! He chose you to be in His family. When we understand this, we will look to adopt others into His love, because our adoption is so valuable to us. I have several friends who are choosing to add to their family by adopting before trying to conceive children biologically, just so their adopted child will know they were chosen.

No one on earth is too far gone, too forsaken, or too old to be adopted by God. God is in the adoption business, and it is His will to increase His family by way of adoption. And God doesn't adopt for surface reasons. He doesn't adopt us only when we behave or have something to contribute to His family. He adopts us out of who He is—constantly loving and pursuing.

Are you living as an adopted son or daughter, or do you feel forsaken or abandoned by God? You are adopted by God, not fostered by God. It is God's delight to set you in His family—and in families here on earth too (Psalm 68:5–6). Maybe you haven't considered yourself to be adopted, but have any old lies or labels kept you from having close relationships? Maybe you've believed you are a burden to others. Maybe you've been told your personality is "too much" or you haven't felt spiritual enough to hang with a particular group of people. If we live by labels, we will keep people at arm's length.

In Christ we find an incredible invitation: we are invited to live, not as abandoned orphans seeking love through perfect performance, but as adopted sons and daughters with a holy heritage—loved and chosen, just as we are.

YOU ARE NAMED "CHOSEN"

My first real job was working for a large nonprofit. I had the opportunity to travel around the country and meet with Christian leaders and organizations. I loved the mission of the organization—to strengthen marriages and families around the world—and I was passionate about the work, considering I had seen firsthand the destruction that takes place when the family unit falls apart.

One of the perks of my job was to attend events representing the organization. There were many Christian conferences and churches I couldn't wait to visit so I could see the body of Christ in action.

One of my favorite conferences invited me to bring some friends with me the following year. I thoroughly enjoy connecting people and love when my friends become friends. I was so excited, and I had no idea how to decide which friends to bring. My top strength on the StrengthsFinder test is inclusiveness, and I absolutely hate leaving people out!

I opted to extend the invitation to a few of my friends in the National Football League—friends I had met through the Ellisses. These players had extensive practice and travel schedules, and this conference took place during their off-season.

We made plans well in advance to attend the conference, and I coordinated all of our travel, lodging, and meals and received backstage passes so I could introduce these friends to nationally respected pastors and leaders.

As soon as we got there, we got separated in the crowd, and I had forgotten to keep a backstage pass for myself. Since this event was in a massive arena, we had no cell phone service. How would we ever find each other now that the service had begun? I knew my friends would be fine, but I didn't want to be left out of the fun.

As I explained my situation to a volunteer, he called me a groupie. He accused me of trying to chase after these players and get access to them and told me I should be more focused on God.

A groupie? I thought to myself. *I've never been called a groupie before. What does he mean by this label?*

I explained that these were friends I had known for years, and that I had arranged for them to be here. I asked if he could help put me in touch with them, but he laughed at me and said I wasn't allowed to be backstage.

Not only did I not feel chosen in that moment, but even worse, I felt forgotten and left behind. I had spent months praying and preparing for this event, and this was *not* the way I envisioned things going.

While not all of us will experience the feeling of being chosen here on earth, we are chosen by God. It's downright odd to see the people God chooses in the Bible. God's chosen ones are not the people we'd think would have all-access badges to our conferences and events. God chooses the least of these. He chooses the overlooked. He chooses us, and in the book of Hosea, we see God choosing a prostitute to become a wife, giving us an example of how we are chosen and renamed.

God tells a man named Hosea to marry a prostitute named Gomer. Out of obedience to God, Hosea marries Gomer, and they have three children together. God tells them to name two of the children Lo-Ruhamah ("not loved") and Lo-Ammi ("not my people"). Between Gomer's prostitute past and having to name their children "Not Loved" and "Not My People," Hosea may have been wondering if these kids were even biologically his own.

Gomer and her children represented Israel's infidelity to God. Israel had turned its back on God, like many of us do today. God's Word is full of examples of individuals and people groups turning their backs on God. Yet the Bible is a love story full of examples of God choosing and pursuing a person to draw them into His family. Israel was prosperous at this time, and its citizens were oppressing the poor. Hosea, which means "salvation," was a prophet who came to speak of God's true characteristics and give us an object lesson of how God pursues us, even in our sin.

God pursued Gomer through Hosea's love, and He went from saying, "You are not my people" (Hosea 1:9), to "You are my people" just one chapter later (2:23).

God chose Israel time and time again, even when they did not choose Him. God chased after Gomer, even while she was chasing after others. And God chooses you, making your new name "Chosen," even when you feel you've made a mess of things.

God remained faithful to Israel and said, "I will plant her for myself in the land; I will show my love to the one I called 'Not my loved one.' I will say to those called 'Not my people,' 'You are my people'; and they will say, 'You are my God'" (Hosea 2:23). God changed their name and called them His own. Every single one of us in the family of God has been chosen and pursued by God.

My friends roamed around the arena to find me and apologized for getting separated. I felt ashamed to express any strong emotions, like sadness or insecurity, because at this time in my life, I avoided conflict at all costs. I felt guilty about standing up for myself and didn't want to come across as too strong, opinionated, assertive, emotional, or attention-seeking. When we live out of old labels, we lack a strong sense of who we are.

Feeling left out triggered my old labels, like "high maintenance" and "not worth the time," and so the deepest part of me felt stuck. It wasn't until I began reflecting on this incident while writing this book that I recognized I wasn't living out of my new name. I had forgotten who I was and to whom I belonged. Old labels can lie to us about ourselves and about other people, and labels can set up lies about God and who He is toward us.

I want us to explore these labels so we no longer live out of them. I don't want painful circumstances to continue to wound the deepest parts of us. I want us to become confident that even if we're left out on earth, we will not be left out in the kingdom of God. Search God's Word for all the ways that God pursues a new name and a new future for people—like Hosea and Gomer, for example—to demonstrate his loving-kindness and faithfulness. There is not a child of God around who is not adopted out of love, chosen and named as His.

YOU ARE NAMED "RIGHTEOUS"

Maybe it was because I didn't have parents who affirmed me, but I never felt good enough. I felt I was never smart enough, compassionate enough, or godly enough to please God. And certain Christian traditions focus on our sins more than others. Many times I found myself in these circles that focused more on our depravity than on God's provision of lifting us out of our misery and making us new creations. This left a deep impression on me—so much so that it was hard to believe God when He called me "righteous."

I had read in Scripture that we are to pursue righteousness (1 Timothy 6:11) and seek righteousness first (Matthew 6:33), but how would I ever accomplish this? Was righteousness about doing the right things or being born into the right family? Was righteousness about being with the right people or having the right answers about God when I was asked?

"Righteous" is a name that belongs to God. He alone is good (Mark 10:18). But Christians are named "Righteous" when we receive Jesus through faith. The apostle Paul wrote, "I consider [all things I have lost] garbage, that I may gain Christ and be found in him, not having a righteousness of my own that comes from the law, but that which is through faith in Christ—the righteousness that comes from God on the basis of faith" (Philippians 3:8–9).

"Righteous" is another new name given to us through faith

alone. It's not a name we deserve, but it's a name that has been bestowed on us.

Righteousness is a big word that means "uprightness." Synonyms for *righteous* are *good, upright, decent,* and *virtuous.* Many rewards come with being righteous (Proverbs 11:18). And even though *righteous* is a big religious word, most of us desire to be in right standing with God.

Peacemakers "reap a harvest of righteousness" (James 3:18), and a righteous person has their prayers heard (5:16). As a high school student, I received an award for "Most Likely to Win a Nobel Peace Prize" for the way I esteemed peace. I didn't realize that making peace in the world was so valued by God! Even as a middle school student and as a new Christian, I wanted God to hear my prayers.

Our new name, "Righteous," is based on what Jesus did on the cross. Righteousness is so less dependent on us than we think! It's not about our actions at all. Every believer is first a sinner, but then a sinner who repents of their actions and takes God up on His free gift of salvation. Sinners can be renamed "Righteous"! That's the story for all of us who look to Christ.

My friend Bonnie has a beautiful heart for people experiencing homelessness. She started a ministry in Salt Lake City to provide food for people who were homeless. It was an honor to serve alongside her when we were roommates and get to know the names of people instead of misjudging them based on their unfortunate circumstances.

What surprised me was the number of people who lived regular lives with regular jobs and yet whose string of bad luck had left them on the streets, without a job or a home. I heard story after story of people whose illness or medical emergency left them poor and no longer able to get by.

I had times growing up in a single-parent home when I felt left out because we couldn't afford things my other friends could. I know what it's like to be labeled "cheap," "poor," and "vulnerable."

But focusing on these labels can cause us to forget how richly God has provided for us: "Command those who are rich in this present world not to be arrogant nor to put their hope in wealth, which is so uncertain, but to put their hope in God, who richly provides us with everything for our enjoyment" (1 Timothy 6:17).

Whether we are rich or poor, we're not to take on those terms as a name or label. I thought serving people who were less fortunate than me would make me righteous, but it turns out that it is not our action or inaction that makes us righteous; it is our faith in Christ alone.

A leader from a different political party than yours can be righteous, just as much as the local pastor you admire can be righteous. We can find righteous friends of different ethnicities and socioeconomic statuses and from different denominations. When we take the name "Righteous," we focus on the work that Christ did for us on the cross, not on our deeds, whether good or bad.

Our new names give us a corporate identity and corporate association too. God clothes us in new robes of righteousness (Isaiah 61:10)—a truth that should cause us to rejoice and want to celebrate with others with this new name! If you knew your name was "Righteous," would you continue to believe that you're unworthy, not good enough, or disappointing to God?

YOU ARE NAMED "ACCEPTED"

Sacred Marriage, written by Gary Thomas, was one of the first Christian books I read on marriage. It's a great book that transformed my view on what marriage is supposed to be. Years later, I met the author and became friends with Gary and his wife, Lisa.

Gary shared with me that he received 120 rejection letters during an eight-year span of trying to get published. He said, "Magazines, publishers, agents—nobody wanted anything I wrote for nearly an entire decade. But I couldn't put all of my heart into anything else."

After eight years of writing with no acceptance in sight, Gary wrote an article for a major magazine, which led to a publisher offering him his first book contract. Having his manuscript and idea accepted was the greatest feeling!

When you and I serve Christ, we become acceptable to God (Romans 14:18). I am so grateful for this acceptance! God makes us insiders and colaborers with Him. Have you ever celebrated being accepted by God?

Sometimes it's easier to remember the 120 rejections we've experienced than to live out of our new name—"Accepted." If we fail to remember this new name, we may be prone to take on a spirit of rejection or despair. But that is not our name! Because of Christ, we are accepted fully, unconditionally, and eternally.

This acceptance doesn't stop with us. Once "Accepted" becomes our new name, we look for ways to accept others in all kinds of ways—from Bonnie's ministry to those experiencing homelessness to a prison ministry that visits people who feel left out and alone. It becomes our job to seek out others and offer them the same acceptance offered to us. Paul urges us, "Accept one another, then, just as Christ accepted you, in order to bring praise to God" (Romans 15:7).

As an accomplished author, Gary has accepted me and encouraged me as a new author. Gary's book has sold more than a million copies in more than fifteen languages, and yet he treats me as a peer. Gary and his wife were some of the most encouraging people during our engagement season and sent us a beautiful wedding gift, congratulating Joel and me for entering into a sacred marriage.

YOU ARE NAMED "LOVED"

This may be the most important name of all. And it has come to be my favorite. Everything rests on knowing and believing this name. This name is central to the Christian faith, to who our God is, and to who we are. We are loved, and we're called this name by a God whose love never ends.

John 3:16 is the famous verse you see on signs at football games or on Tim Tebow's eye black. Many of us memorize this verse early on in our Christian walk: "For God so loved the world that he gave his one and only Son, that whoever believes in him shall not perish but have eternal life" (John 3:16). And what follows is just as important: "For God did not send his Son into the world to condemn the world, but to save the world through him."

Having traveled the world and met people from different cultures and different generations, I think it's fair to say that most of us, more often than not, feel more condemned than we feel loved. Most of us struggle with inadequacy rather than bask in an overflow of love and acceptance. But this is the polar opposite of who God says we are. God says we are loved, and He loved us so much that He gave us Jesus. This makes us receivers of love and grace, of mercy and strength, and because He loves us, we receive everything we need to live a godly life (2 Peter 1:3).

My earliest memories are of believing that something was deeply wrong with me. I saw myself as the common denominator for why people left me, abused me, and blamed me for their problems. I was ashamed and distrusted everyone—including myself. By God's grace and a decade or so of counseling, I was able to give my heart in marriage to Joel.

But I was still scared. I was waiting for the other shoe to drop and was sure my deepest fear of abandonment would come true. I inappropriately felt I deserved brokenness because I took this on as my label and story. God does not want us to live in inner turmoil. This kind of existence is not free, abundant living; it's what living out of fear and wrong labels looks like. God was challenging my doom-and-gloom outlook.

Was brokenheartedness what God desired for me? Certainly not! Was divorce or abandonment God's perfect will for my marriage? No! So as I asked God to show me my new name and what He wanted for me, I began to see myself and my marriage differently. Marriage was becoming a channel for my healing rather than giving me another broken label that would cause me pain.

How would allowing people to love us change the way we see ourselves? And we don't need to have a spouse to be loved. In fact, dozens of people tried to love me before I was ever married, but unfortunately I limited these relationships because I was believing the lie behind the label "unloved." Believing labels prevents us from receiving unconditional love. Hiding behind labels limits relationships and keeps people from knowing us for who we truly are. How would believing your name is "Loved" change the way you live? How would becoming love to others, which starts with believing it for ourselves, change the culture around us?

What names resonate with you? God your Father has called you a friend (John 15:15). Do you feel you can say that about Him? These new names are yours for the taking. Which new name can you discover for yourself? God desperately wants to give you a new name and make it personal to you. Getting a new name is part of your testimony. What name can you begin to live out of?

All of these beautiful names listed above are only the beginning. God calls us so many more names in Scripture. We believe these words by faith and by reading them in God's Word. People could tell me all day long that I was loved, but it wasn't until I heard it from God that I was changed. Learning our new names may take only a moment, but *believing* our new names is the project of a lifetime. Do you believe God wants to speak a loving new name and identity over you? Can you get alone with God and ask Him to help you believe what He says about you?

Are we focusing on the name God calls us, or are we listening to the world around us? Do we know the truth because we bathe ourselves in Scripture and see the good and bad inside us, or are we letting our culture name us? God will often use people around us to help us see a clearer picture of who we are. This is why choosing our friends, our church, or our spouse is so important. The people in our community will either confirm who we are in Christ or confuse us.

We can stop living with a fake ID and rely on our new name. As the apostle John wrote, "And so we know and rely on the love God has for us" (1 John 4:16). We can rely on God's love because God's love is unchanging. God will never tell us to be or become something that He is not. We love because He is love. We are to be holy because He is holy. We give because He gave, and we can rely on the love of God because He is love: "God is love. Whoever lives in love lives in God, and God in them" (1 John 4:16).

Sometimes when I forget who I am, I go to the Word of God—the most reliable mirror we can ever find, always ready to remind us of who God is and who we are as His image bearers. How we see ourselves is often shaped by what church we go to. Some churches focus on who we are becoming, forgetting our past and our need for God; other churches focus on the past, forgetting who we are becoming. For example, it would be easy to focus on seeing ourselves like Hosea—the ones who love the unlovable. But we are also Gomer—the ones who forget the love that has beautifully pursued us and who choose other loves.

When we focus on God, we will hear both names, but we live out of our new name. We are keenly aware of our ability to sin, our wretchedness, and our desperate need for God in every moment of every day, while simultaneously believing we are loved, chosen, accepted, and named by God. We are to live out of who God says we are and who He is calling us to be.

When I get a clearer picture of who I am, I'm prepared for whatever comes my way. When the world around me says I'm not loved, I know different. When I'm not chosen by the right boss or the right publisher, it will be okay, because I know that God chooses me. Knowing our name plays a key role in how we persevere in a culture that is constantly calling us names.

As you consider your own life, do you sense you've focused more on your old names than your new? Does your belief system leave room for God to rename you? Do you believe God has the ability out of His love for you to rename you? You can start by opening the Word of God to hear what He says about you. His names will be far better than any you could give to yourself. Once you discover His name for you, it will become as familiar as your physical name and will be something you can rely on for years to come.

For Further Reflection

Reflection: Out of all the new names mentioned in chapters 2 and 3 ("Disciple," "God's Handiwork," "Imitator of God," "God's Instrument," "Saint," "Ambassador," "Farmer," "Fisher of People," "Minister," "Christian," "Follower of the Way," "Son," "Daughter," "Adopted," "Chosen," "Accepted," "Righteous," "Loved"), which new name sticks out to you? With whom can you begin to process your new name?

Prayer of Faith: Heavenly Father, help me to have faith without doubt when it comes to who You say I am. Allow me to hear life-giving words from You, even when my circumstances are difficult. Give me a new confidence to live as Your child and not as my former self. In Jesus' name I pray. Amen.

Verses to Believe: Matthew 21:21; James 1:6

Labels That Limit
Circle which of the old labels you have believed about yourself.

Burdensome	Inadequate
Cheap	Insecure
Damaged	Kicked Out
Fearful	Left Behind
Forgotten	Not Good Enough
Foster Child	Not Loved
Groupie	Not My Loved One
High Maintenance	Not My People
Homeless	Not Spiritual Enough

Not Worth the Time

Overlooked

Poor

Prostitute

Rejected

Sad

Servant (can be both positive
    and negative!)

Slave

Too Much

Undeserving

Unwed Pregnant Teen

Vulnerable

Worrier

Your New Name

Circle which of the new names you want to live out of.

Accepted

Adopted

Belong

Blessed

Chosen

Christian

Colaborer

Counted

Daughter/Son/Child of God

Favored

Follower of the Way

Friend of God

Heir

Holy Heritage

Insider

Little Christ

Loved

My People

Older Sister

Peacemaker

Provided For

Receiver of God's Good Gifts

Receiver of Mercy and
    Strength

Righteous

Seen

We Have Everything
    We Need

Wife/Husband

CHAPTER 4

Getting Unstuck from Your Past

*"Don't call me Naomi," she told them. "Call me Mara,
because the Almighty has made my life very bitter."*
RUTH 1:20

Early on in our dating period, I asked Joel about his military experience. He served as a captain in the United States Air Force and was stationed in Washington State, Qatar, and Germany. After living for years in Colorado Springs, I had several friends in the military, and the air base he was stationed at sounded particularly familiar to me. I began asking questions. "How long were you there? What was it like? What did you do when you were there?"

I was trying to figure out if any of my friends had served with him.

As Joel and I continued talking, I glanced down and saw my silver bracelet, the one I wore in memory of Captain David I. Lyon—my friend from my church in Colorado who was in the Air Force and was killed in action by a roadside bomb just two days after Christmas. It was just days before the one-year anniversary of David's death, and emotions stirred as Joel began to talk about his military career.

This terrorist attack ended David's life as he was leaving the base in the Middle East where he and his wife, Captain Dana Lyon, were stationed. They were two of my best friends at church, and I could hardly believe it had been almost a year since David had gone to be with Jesus.

Distracted, I interrupted one of Joel's stories and asked, "Did you by any chance know David Lyon while you were in the Air Force?"

I knew there were thousands of people in the Air Force, but it was worth asking.

Joel paused. "Was he also married to a captain in the Air Force?" he replied.

My eyes grew wide, and I leaned in. "Yes," I said eagerly.

Joel began to tell me about the time he met David's wife, Dana, who was accompanying David's body back to the United States. Joel told me it was rare to see an officer accompany their spouse's body, and it was memorable.

Joel proceeded to tell me he was stationed at Ramstein Air Base in Germany at the time of David's death. One of his jobs was to ensure that our military men and women who were killed in action received a dignified transfer. He and his team had seen hundreds of soldiers come through this base throughout the course of a year, and David and his wife were two of the people he remembered.

Joel worked hard to ensure that Dana was looked after. He remembered telling his team to take extra care of Captain Dana Lyon, as she would be returning without her husband by her side. I sat there in shock that this man I hardly knew had been on the other side of the world caring for my friend before he even knew me.

GOD IS IN THE DETAILS

God is always working out the details of our lives. We just rarely see Him at work. He is not surprised by any twist or turn in our lives. He is a God who holds the universe together, while simultaneously knitting us together in our mothers' wombs and holding our tiny human hearts. I had never seen the God of details as clearly as I did that day.

One year prior, when I had received word that David was killed, I immediately left my respite season in Alaska to fly to Colorado Springs, where Dana was bringing David home. David and Dana were two of my very best friends. Through Dana's grief, she taught me how to pray the beautiful prayer of lament in her deepest time of need. Instead of cursing at God or turning against Him, Dana showed me how to pray and lament to God. She cried out to Him, wept, and wailed. She was filled with grief but didn't isolate herself in her time of need. Through Dana, I got a glimpse of how God stands close by those who are brokenhearted. As I went to Colorado to prepare Dana's home for her return, I prayed that God would send good people to her until I could see her face-to-face.

Before Dana arrived home, I went to every room in her house and prayed. I fasted for her safe return and prayed that she would not grieve without hope. I wanted her heart to be comforted, but I also wanted her to be protected and provided for. The prayer I repeated the most was, "God, please send good people to Dana to comfort her, to protect her, to ensure that she gets home safely."

I prayed and prayed and prayed. I wanted Dana to remember God in her storm.

I'll never forgot these prayers, because I pleaded with God in them. In my friend's darkest hour, I wanted God to show Himself to her through the presence of others. Little did I know that God was using my future husband as an answer to these prayers. Just days shy of the one-year mark of David's death, I was sitting across the table from a man who was an answer to prayer for my friend, not knowing he would later become an answer to prayer for me as well.

One of the most difficult things we go through on this side of heaven is the feeling of being alone. Whether you are married, single, divorced, widowed, in a difficult marriage, or surrounded by people and yet feeling misunderstood, feeling alone is miserable. And even though David, the love of Dana's life, was now in heaven, I hoped that meeting good people like Joel would remind Dana that God had never left her side.

As I sat across from this man I barely knew, I respected him more than words could express. He was the one God sent for Dana in her time of need. He honored David's life by the way he treated Dana. As Joel shared with me that he commanded his support staff to surround Dana with extra support and to take care of her needs, I knew that if God was in *these* details, He would be in the details of my life too.

GOD CARES FOR WIDOWS

As I sat next to Dana during each memorial service for her fallen husband, I noticed that a few people used the name "Widow," and it just felt too soon. Dana had hardly had time to adapt to her new reality of being alone. I remember getting upset with people who would use the "W" word for my friend, who wasn't even thirty years old. But over time, I've seen how God has taken great care of widows and widowers and how He has a special place in His heart for them. God tells us to look after widows in their distress (James 1:27), and throughout the Bible, He gives examples of brave men and women who have made their Maker their spouse in a time of loss (Isaiah 54:4–5).

The book of Ruth is a story about three widows and how God cared for them. A woman named Naomi—as well as her daughters-in-law, Ruth and Orpah—had been widowed. Their story unfolded during the period of the judges in the Bible. To give you an indication of the times they were living in, the last line in the book of Judges reads, "In those days there was no king in Israel. Everyone did what was right in his own eyes" (Judges 21:25 ESV). Sounds eerily similar to our current day, doesn't it?

Ruth reminds us of God's providence in the midst of tragedy. We all need this hope in our lives, especially when tragedy shows up in our own homes. I'm amazed at the care and concern God has for women throughout Scripture. The book of Ruth shows us God's care and concern for individual women. It shows us that God is in the details, even when we may feel He has lost sight of us.

After watching Dana enter a season without her husband, I read the book of Ruth through a different lens. Not only were the majority of people living in that time disobedient to God, but the land was also experiencing a famine. These were desolate times, and God showed His involvement on earth through the lives of these widows. Ruth was from Moab, a nation that was politically at odds with Israel. So the fact that the Hebrew Scriptures dedicated an entire book to this woman's name and story is remarkable. We see in this story how God cares about women, widows, and immigrants.

As we look at the book of Ruth, we see how much Ruth valued relationships. Not only did she decide to live with her mother-in-law in a new land after her husband died, but her move also signified that she had chosen a relationship with Naomi's God—Yahweh, the God of the Bible.

Very little is told about Orpah, Ruth's sister-in-law. Ruth and Orpah both became widows. Naomi, their mother-in-law, desired to release Ruth and Orpah from the requirements of an Israelite household when she told them to go back to their land. Scholars say it's not that Naomi didn't want them close; it's that she wanted to release them to be free and possibly even to marry again. Naomi was just as heartbroken as Orpah and Ruth, as she too had lost her spouse. Maybe Naomi wanted them to find love again, which is a selfless thing for a mother-in-law to desire.

Orpah and Ruth chose different paths. Orpah kissed her mother-in-law goodbye, and Ruth clung to Naomi (Ruth 1:14).

Orpah did not choose wrongly. The Bible doesn't say she left angry or bitter; it doesn't really tell us much of anything at all. Yet I admire Ruth for following the God of Israel and going to a new land.

YOUR NEW NAME AFTER TRAGEDY STRIKES

After Joel and I began dating in Oxford, he asked me if I would consider moving to his home state so we could continue getting to know one another. While I was reluctant to move for a man I had just met, I wanted to get to know him better as well, so I agreed. My decision was a shock to me just as much as it was to those who knew me.

Truth be told, I was a bit embarrassed to be moving for a dating relationship. It was scary and required faith that God would show me what was next if this relationship didn't work out. But this was a new land, unfamiliar to me, and it was a hot land. I didn't think my skin would survive Texas's blistering temperatures.

The move was hard and had its challenges. Not only was the temperature something I had never experienced before, but my allergies were bad, and I had no friends to go to dinner with or process our dating relationship with in person. When we follow God to a new land, beautiful things are on the other side of our obedience, but those things don't always come easily. Following God requires us to overcome fear and the contentment of living comfortably in our old names and labels.

Sometimes God will call us to stay, and sometimes He'll call us to go. There won't be a cookie-cutter plan for any of us, because God desires an individual relationship with us and makes us all unique. He knows the details of our life stories and customizes seasons of growth for each of us. Our walk with God should have movement to it. There ought to be new things God is saying to us and calling us to. We are not designed to stay still in our walk with God. Ask God to help you choose the best path, not the easiest one. Ask Him to give you the feet to handle whatever path He puts you on. And ask Him to help you make decisions by faith in order to please Him (Hebrews 11:6).

There's no doubt in my mind that Ruth had challenges in this new land. She had a labor-intensive job of gleaning fields behind the harvesters (Ruth 2:7). Ruth was working hard and showing consistency, but I imagine she was tired at the end of these long days, and sad and lonely after losing her husband. I bet there were days when she felt her hope was cut off.

Our character is revealed during our times of crisis and need. Orpah went back to the familiar, her hometown, and Ruth walked in faith to a new land. Naomi, Ruth's mother-in-law, fell into the trap of bitterness, which many of us fall into during seasons of grief. Discovering our new name will have a lot to do with which road we choose to take. How have you dealt with bitter circumstances in your life?

BITTER CIRCUMSTANCES

Naomi had faced several hardships. She went from being married and probably financially secure to returning to Israel as a widow and being poor. There's a reason Scripture tells us to care for widows in their distress (James 1:27), since it was hard for a woman, especially in ancient times, to recover financially after losing her spouse. Naomi was a foreigner without a husband and without sons. Scripture reveals the many times she wept (Ruth 1.9, 14).

Naomi responded to these circumstances in a way many of us would. She renamed herself: "'Don't call me Naomi,' she told them. 'Call me Mara, because the Almighty has made my life very bitter'" (Ruth 1:20).

Naomi identified so deeply with her bitterness that she took it on as a name. We must be careful about the names we attach to ourselves when we're sad, lonely, hurting, and grieving. Naomi renamed herself based on her circumstances, not on who she was in God.

The name Naomi means "pleasant," and she wanted to be renamed Mara, meaning "bitter." Naomi saw herself as bitter and took this on as a name and identity, diminishing the sweet fragrance her Hebrew name exhibited. In other words, she exchanged her God-given name for the name dictated to her by her circumstances.

How many of us have renamed ourselves in the midst of a trial? Perhaps we've taken on qualities like "bitter" and "resentful," or maybe we've let "Victim," "Abused," or "Neglected" become our new name. We can stay stuck and paralyzed if we name ourselves based on our grief. How many of us have renamed ourselves "Unworthy" and "Unloved" or been so heartbroken that we made a vow to never again open ourselves up to love?

When we rename ourselves based on our circumstances, we're taking our eyes off our Creator and the larger story of our life that extends past the tragedy we may be experiencing. No one would blame Naomi for being bitter. Her circumstances were devastating, but God did not give this new name to Naomi. He did not wish bitterness on her, and He wanted to be bigger to her than what was right in front of her.

I get it. Sometimes awful circumstances seem to surround us more than the reality of God. But be careful not to take on a new name in these seasons. We will face similar options as we respond to the storms in life. Will we respond like Orpah and go back to the familiar? Will we respond like Ruth and follow God to unknown places? Or will we be like Naomi and name ourselves based on our bitter circumstances?

I see no place in Scripture where we are given permission to rename ourselves. Instead, I see it is God who renames us. God gives us new names through Scripture, and He also has a new name saved up for us in heaven. Are you bitter because of your circumstances? Have you allowed these painful experiences to name you? Have you identified with these labels to the point that they are louder than the names God lovingly speaks over you?

Not only will pain hit our lives, but we will cause others pain too. When we've done wrong to others, have we given this sin permission to rename us? Do we call ourselves "One Who Messed Up" or "Failure" or "One Who Never Gets Things Right"? Yet if we've truly repented from our sinful choices or behavior, we must not take this sin on and rename ourselves because of it. We are not our sin, just as we are not our good deeds.

None of us who have turned away from our sin should be renamed by it. None of us should be consigned to the labels of our actions. We are so much more than our addictions, our achievements, our mistakes, our accidents. We are not defined by our struggles, our appearance, our failures, or our secrets. Here is the question: Are we willing to listen to how God sees us?

WHERE TO FIND STRENGTH AS YOU WAIT FOR YOUR NEW NAME

As Ruth continued to glean in the fields, a man named Boaz noticed her (Ruth 2:5). Boaz's name means "In him is strength." I see several parallels between Boaz and God.

- Boaz was a man of wealth (2:1), and God owns the cattle on a thousand hills (Psalm 50:10).
- Boaz was gracious in speech and greeted others (2:4), and the Lord is gracious in speech and cares that we speak graciously to others (Colossians 4:6).
- Boaz inquired about Ruth (2:5), and the Lord inquires about people (Genesis 3:9).
- Boaz took measures to protect Ruth (2:9, 15), and God protects us (2 Thessalonians 3:3).
- Boaz quenched Ruth's thirst (2:9), and Jesus is the living water in whom we will never thirst again (John 4; 7).

These cues in the text all reveal a bigger story at work. Boaz is called a "guardian-redeemer" (Ruth 3:9), which refers to a close relative who can act on behalf of members of the extended family who are in crisis. God constantly acts on our behalf when we are in trouble and need help (Genesis 48:16; Exodus 6:6), and He redeems us (Leviticus 25:47–55; 27:9–25).

Throughout Scripture, God describes Himself as our strength: "The LORD is my strength and my shield" (Psalm 28:7); "God is our refuge and strength, an ever-present help in trouble" (Psalm 46:1). God wants to be our strength in the midst of hardship, and the story of Boaz is a reminder of this truth.

Though it isn't said, I can imagine that part of Naomi's grief over the death of her sons came from the fact that she wouldn't get the chance to become a grandmother. There is present pain from the loss of a loved one, as well as the future pain of grieving hopes and dreams that will not come true.

God didn't end either Naomi's or Ruth's story with death. These women were bold, brave, and tenacious. They had to persevere through a lot of hardship, but it wasn't the end of their stories. Ruth married Boaz and became a mother, signifying new birth after a storm. Against all odds, this new life made Naomi a grandmother. And from what I hear, becoming a grandparent is pretty "pleasant"—the original meaning of Naomi's name. Grief wasn't the end of their stories, nor will it be the end of yours.

I encourage you not to rename yourself prematurely. Seasons will change. Blessings will come again. Naomi's life did not stay bitter forever, and neither will yours. Think of what Naomi would have missed out on if she had refused to let hope reenter her heart.

God does not want you to rename yourself based on your painful circumstances or on the worst thing that has ever happened to you. He loves you too much, and He will be your guardian-redeemer to get you through the storm. He has a better name for you than a name based on your bitter circumstances.

God watches over Dana—I'm sure of it. While her grief is real and ongoing, she has not given up. Dana has not renamed herself "Bitter"; rather, she is giving back and mentoring cadets at the Air Force Academy, where she now works. Dana is called "Coach," "Mentor," and "Mama" by dozens of student athletes. In addition to her job, Dana is fighting for widows at the Pentagon level who have lost their spouses and need a defender. I know God arises to defend widows (Exodus 22:22) because of how God has loved and protected Dana.

God watches over widows (Psalm 146:9), and He wants them to hope in Him (1 Timothy 5:3–16) and not rename themselves in their pain. Dana will always miss David. His name will forever be a part of her story. But God isn't through writing Dana's story here on earth. And He isn't through writing your story either. How will you respond to the storms in life? Waiting on God for your new name will put God on display: "Then the women said to Naomi, 'Blessed be the LORD, who has not left you this day without a redeemer, and may his name be renowned in Israel!'" (Ruth 4:14 ESV).

We do not have to lose our name or identity when the worst of circumstances happens to us. Instead, we can fight on, wait in hope, and ask God to give us a new season and a new name. His desire is to restore us, not have us crumble under the pressure, anxiety, and grief of this life.

YOUR NEW NAME IS YOUR TESTIMONY

Evangelist Christine Caine is a woman of God on a mission. Christine and her husband, Nick, run Equip and Empower Ministries and started the anti–human trafficking group called the A21 Campaign. The A21 Campaign has twelve offices across the globe. Its mission has to do with awareness raising, prevention, and protection, as well as prosecution of traffickers.

Christine is the most power-packed woman I've ever met. She is passionate, down to earth, faith-filled, and approachable. Our paths first crossed at the Catalyst Conference, a conference for young leaders, when Christine was about to speak to fourteen thousand church leaders.

Without knowing Christine, it would be easy to see her ministry, book sales, or organizational success and think her life is a breeze. But when Christine took the stage at the Catalyst Conference, she began by telling people that the name given to her on her birth certificate was "Unnamed."

I was stunned. Christine grew up in Australia and was raised by Greek Orthodox parents. She didn't find out she was adopted until later in life, and when she did, she did some research and found out her original name was "Unnamed."

Can you imagine that? It's hard to fathom until we think about all the pregnancies for which we use the term *unwanted*.

Unnamed?

Unwanted?

Unadoptable?

These labels can stick with us, and they hurt. By God's strength, "Unnamed" didn't stay that way. She was chosen, adopted, and given the beautiful name of Christine. Later God provided a godly husband for Christine Caryofyllis, and she became Christine Caine. By God's kindness, Christine Caine preaches the gospel to the nations. By God's justice, God uses her to help free trafficking victims around the globe. As hard as it was to find out her first birth name, she did not let this label define her.

You don't have to stay unnamed. You don't have to stay afraid, rejected, or insecure. Painful things happen to us, but we don't have to be defined by them. Christine fought to become the woman God made her to be, and now she is fighting for others to be renamed by God. Interestingly enough, the name Christine means "follower of Christ." Talk about living up to her God-given name! When God renames us, we become new. With that transformation come a courage and joy to tell others what He has done for us! God is transforming you. Can you see it?

For Further Reflection

Reflection: What circumstance from your past threatens to identify you? How have you renamed yourself based on that circumstance instead of waiting on God for your new name? What labels have you gleaned from your circumstance and allowed to identify you? What true names is God replacing those labels with?

Prayer of Repentance: Lord, where my life has been bitter, help me see You as pleasant and sweet. I want to taste and see that You are good. Please open my eyes to see Your kindness. Produce good fruit inside me. Forgive me when I have incorrectly named myself. Forgive me when I have called myself a name different from the name You have called me. Purify my mind and give me hope and a future. In Jesus' name. Amen.

Verses to Believe: Isaiah 43:19; Jeremiah 2:13; 1 Timothy 5:3

Labels That Limit

Circle which of the old labels you have believed about yourself.

Abused	Heartbroken
Abuser	Murderer
Addict	Neglected
Adulterer	One Who Messed Up/Never
Alcoholic	Gets Things Right
Bitter	Resentful
Divorced	Thief
Failure	Unadoptable

Unloved	Unworthy
Unnamed	Victim
Unwanted	Widow/er

Your New Name

Circle which of the new names you want to live out of.

Coach	Remembered by God
Hopeful	Seen by God
Mentor	Spiritual Parent

CHAPTER 5

Wrestling between Names

Then the man said, "Your name will no longer be Jacob,
but Israel, because you have struggled with God and with
humans and have overcome."
GENESIS 32:28

After my biological father died, Joel and I had to decide whether we would attend the funeral. Part of me wanted to go—mostly out of obligation and a desire to be a good daughter, a Christian daughter who honors her earthly parents. Part of me wondered if attending his funeral and seeing him one last time would provide me any healing or closure.

My practical side didn't think I could even make it through booking a ticket without having a panic attack. My father left our family decades prior and never bothered saying goodbye or staying in touch. It would have felt weird and out of place to go. His appearances in my life were spontaneous and sporadic as his mental illness got the best of him. It's hard to know how to grieve the death of a parent when they've been absent long before they physically leave the earth.

I wrestled with this decision. I grieved the fact that I didn't want to go and that I felt uncomfortable going. Did this make me a bad daughter or a bad Christian? Would I come to regret not going one day?

My husband and I decided we would be able to best honor my absent father by ensuring he had a proper burial. Jesus physically rose from the grave, and so there's something symbolic to our physical bodies being buried and waiting for Christ's return.

I endured more grief surrounding my father's death than I anticipated. Truthfully, I cried and cried. I had cried decades earlier when he left our family. Then in the early courtroom appearances I cried, and later as a child during supervised visitations. I didn't think I had any tears left. But here I was, sitting with my new husband, the man of my dreams, crying as I made our dinners, crying as I folded laundry, crying as I lay my head on my pillow at night. Esther Fleece was hurting deeply, even when Esther Allen was who I was trying to become. And in many ways, I grieved leaving my old name behind. Some of us will have to say goodbye to old names we loved and old ways we used to live. Old identities feel familiar and comfortable to us, even if God is calling us to new identities.

Living out of our new names doesn't mean we cut out painful labels of the past quickly. Even though many of us want our new names to erase our old lives, our new names are meant to put the emphasis on God and what He has done inside us. Thus, painful parts of our stories are required. Our old names don't just go away, even if our new names come overnight.

Whether I liked it or not, grief was the appropriate emotion after my father's death. I was a very happy bride and simultaneously a very sad daughter. There will be circumstances in life that cause us to wrestle with our new names. Do we give ourselves grace and space for God to do a transforming work inside us? Do we allow those around us to have different stories of transformation from the ones we have?

I found great healing in counseling, and some will find it in journaling or support group meetings. I needed a place to process my disappointments and grief, and I needed someone to tell me it was okay to not be okay. After years of chugging along and putting on my happy face, I needed to know it was okay to be sad and to grieve that I was not going to have reconciliation on this side of heaven with my biological dad.

I experienced the love of God through the love of my spouse, but some of the best people I know will never marry. I had to forgive my biological parents without ever hearing an "I'm sorry," but some parents and children will be reconciled.

Life is complex, and so are our stories and emotions. How do we wrestle in faith with God for our new names instead of wrestling against others or trying to prove ourselves to those around us? I was so tired of having to prove myself. When I was kicked out of my home as a youth, I had to prove I wasn't as bad as my mother said I was. When I was stalked by my father, I had to prove to the Christian community that I wasn't a bad daughter for not visiting him in jail. It's a much better use of our time to wrestle with God than to try to prove ourselves to those around us.

Wrestling with God is not only allowed—it's often essential in the process of discovering our new names. My wrestling meant I needed to take a time-out. I needed to scale back my speaking schedule and get time away from work to hear what God was saying to me instead of avoiding the wrestling and staying in my old name.

Why is the wrestling necessary? Because an identity change is intensely personal. It cannot come from afar. Transformation cannot come through looking at Instagram feeds. It's a gift that can only be received up close and personal and by stepping away from the noise of the world and quieting our souls to hear the voice of God.

WRESTLING WITH GOD OVER YOUR NEW NAME

Though I would never hear an "I'm sorry" from my dad, I had to wrestle with God over his death. Though my father and I would never be reconciled on earth, I had to fight to learn how to live out of my new name—"Beloved Daughter." I had to struggle with my true identity. I was still a saint if I put up boundaries. I was still the aroma of Christ when I avoided toxic relationships. Discovering our new names may not be easy, and it may require wrestling with God.

In the Old Testament, we read of a man named Jacob—the son of Isaac and Rebekah and the grandson of Abraham. Jacob and his twin brother, Esau, had a contentious relationship due to the way Jacob treated him.

In the Hebrew language, names may have several meanings. Genesis 27:36 says about Jacob, "Isn't he rightly named Jacob? This is the second time he has taken advantage of me: He took my birthright, and now he's taken my blessing!" This leads many to believe Jacob's original name could mean "he deceives" and even "he cheats." This name fits, since Jacob stole his twin brother Esau's birthright (25:29–34), which signified position and inheritance in the Old Testament. Jacob schemed against people and planned things out to his own advantage.

When Jacob was named in Genesis 25:26, however, the Hebrew uses a root word that means "heel." Sigal Zohar, a professor of Hebrew language at Haifa University, explains that many Hebrew words take their meaning from what is happening around them.[5] Some of the meanings deriving from the Hebrew root meaning "heel" are "to hamper," "to betray," and "to strike someone on the heel." So Jacob's name could have more nuance to it than simply "he deceives." Scholars hold different views on this.

While Jacob was a significant person in the Old Testament, his reputation was not built on his solid character. Jacob stole his brother Esau's birthright and blessing. Imagine how angry you'd be if your sibling stole everything you had! Esau had every right to be upset, and he vowed to kill his brother after their father, Isaac, died (Genesis 27:41). This sibling rivalry was intense, and while I don't want to make Jacob out to be the poster child for wrestling with God, Jacob teaches us how we can contend with God for our new names.

HOW TO WRESTLE WITH GOD

Jacob and his family are on the run because Esau is out to get him. Jacob arrives at the place where they would spend the night. In great distress, Jacob separated his family into two different camps to protect them in case of ambush. Even though we may have some sympathy for what this family is enduring, we're reminded that Jacob's sin of stealing got them into this mess to begin with.

After Jacob puts his family to bed, he goes outside and begins to pray. Jacob acknowledges God and shows gratitude to Him (Genesis 32:9–10), and he asks God to save him and spare his children (32:11). These are good prayers, honoring prayers, and, to be honest, prayers that seem a little safe. There are times I need to ask God for something, but I simply settle for a shout-out or a quick word of praise before bed. But God wants us to approach Him and ask Him for things.

Jacob's prayers eventually begin to get more desperate. And that's when he starts wrestling with God. His wrestling ultimately lasts throughout the night. He is at his emotional end.

Have you ever been there? At the end of your rope? Feeling like your prayers have run out?

During this wrestling match, God asks Jacob, "What is your name?" (Genesis 32:27). As soon as Jacob answers God, God gives him a new name: "Your name will no longer be Jacob, but Israel, because you have struggled with God and with humans and have overcome" (32:28).

Our wrestling with God, our laments, and our questions are not bad things in God's sight. God is not hindered or intimidated by our investigations of Him. On the contrary, wrestling with God can show that we are in relationship with Him. Wrestling sometimes leads us to our new names.

What strikes me is that Jacob sinned. Big-time. But this is not how Jacob is renamed or remembered. Jacob is remembered for being persistent in his wrestling. He wrestles with God through-out the night and finally says, "I will not let you go unless you bless me" (Genesis 32:26). He must be confident in his personal relationship with God to pray such a prayer!

Despite Jacob's many character flaws and despite his sin, the Lord blessed him (Genesis 30:25–40; 31:9) and gave him a new name.

Do we approach God with this kind of confidence? Do we ask God to bless us and give us a new name? Do we expect Him to meet us and change us?

While we often want God to change a circumstance or another person, what happens many times is that our wrestling changes us. It's in the wrestling that God speaks to us, convicts us, or sets us free. In these wrestling seasons, endurance is the name of the game. Jacob endured the wrestling and found his new name at the end.

Likewise, as we remain in relationship with God, even in the wrestling, He changes us!

GOD INVITES US TO GET HONEST

We will all wrestle with our identity, and asking questions is one of the ways God uses to move us to reflect on the label we are living out of. Jacob is asked, "What is your name?" because it's important for him to confess where he is at in life. The Bible includes story after story of God asking His people simple yet pointed questions to let them speak for themselves—questions like,

What is your name? What have you done? Why are you hiding? In God's compassion, He doesn't condemn us. He lets us answer for ourselves. If we listen, God continues to ask us these questions as an invitation to get honest both with Him and with ourselves. God knows exactly what to ask us to cause us to think of Him.

In this story, even before Jacob fully repents, God rewards Jacob's honesty. Jacob didn't have time to get into the right Bible study, attend a Christian university, or clean up his vocabulary before receiving his new name. We don't see until later that Jacob and Esau weep and become reconciled. Jacob receives a new name even before his actions are repentant and righteous. Jacob's name changed to Israel, meaning "he struggles with God," because he struggled with God and *yet* overcame (Genesis 32:28).

We are given new names because we are sons and daughters. Our faith walk will involve wrestling, waiting, questioning, answering, and, yes, asking and receiving. Arguably three of the most important Old Testament figures—Abraham, Isaac, and Jacob—were not given significance in standing because they were perfect. On the contrary, they all were flawed human beings who were honest with God, and God purposed to make them new.

Jacob receives his new name at his point of honesty, and in the same way, our honest plea to God will come with great reward. Jacob was persistent. He didn't give up in his wrestling, and he didn't give up on God. As Jacob wrestled, he refused to quit, and he was given a new name.

Are we familiar with God's character in our wrestling seasons? Many of us have struggled with the name "Doubter" or "Seeker," or maybe we're a question asker who doesn't feel comfortable questioning the things of God in church. God does not define us by our doubts or fears. God not only sees our sin and shame through the cross of Jesus Christ, but takes on our striving as well. His striving is through service and surrender, and we can take on this same posture. We don't have to strive for acceptance anymore.

We can be like Jacob and wrestle with God, getting a new name even before our circumstances change. And remember, if God asks you the question, "Where are you?" be honest!

Can we tell God which label we've held on to for years? Can we tell Him why we feel embarrassed to pray to Him? Can we confess our unbelief or lack of joy? And after doing so, can we start to believe the best about God? When we live *into* this new name we've been given, we can become more like our God-given identity through His strength and pursuit of us.

God knew my heart was breaking over the death of my earthly father, but simultaneously God had already given me a new name. It's something like this: Before I could "prove" to Joel that I would be a good wife, he chose me to be his wife. Long before Joel saw me as Esther Allen, he chose to believe I would carry his name well.

God sees us that same way. Even as I wrestled to fully forgive my abusers, God attached His covenant love to me and gave me strength to forgive. Even as I wrestled with anger and resentment over not being the favored one in the family, God gave me an identity and inheritance in Him (Ephesians 1:11–17). God has an everlasting covenant of love, forgiveness of sins, and eternal inheritance for those of us who have a new covenant name in Him. This might not look like a physical name change, but it will always be a spiritual one, as we show evidence of a changed lifestyle and devotion to God.

The late theologian R. C. Sproul taught that Jacob's new name Israel "loosely means 'El (God) fights.'" Sproul goes on to write, "Jacob's new name hints at this future, but we are also told he is called *Israel* because he has prevailed in his struggle with God and men."[6]

Your new name will hint at your future. God does not abandon us in our wrestling, but we are to persevere, sometimes throughout the night, and keep our faith until the end. So many of us are tempted to give up in the wrestling. We're tired, or perhaps we feel like our faith is too weak. Many of us are afraid to bring our questions to God, and so we miss out on the intimacy-building tool of wrestling.

If we knew our new name was on the other side of the wrestling, would we be more apt to persevere? If I'm running a race, I'm motivated to continue running if I know there's a hot breakfast and cheering friends at the finish line. How much more waits at the end for those who wrestle toward faith!

Scripture rarely talks about struggling without also talking about persevering. Not only are we to hold on to our faith; there may be a new name for us on the other side. All of us have to prevail through harsh circumstances, unkind people, and even the ugly consequences of our own sins. The question is: Are we wrestling with God on the path to becoming more like Him, or are we wrestling against Him in an attempt to push Him away?

Are there old names you're holding on to, like "Hypercritical" or "Anxious" or "Judgmental"? Are there things in your past for which you find it hard to forgive yourself? Have you become known for your mistakes rather than your potential? There will be so many times when we will be tempted to incorrectly name ourselves or give up. The question is not *"Will* this happen to me?" but "When it does, how will I respond?" Will we wrestle with God to discover the new name He gives to us, or will we settle for less?

NEW EYES TO SEE

My friend Bruce saw his first pornographic image at the age of eight. He was at a neighbor's house, and his friend, who was a few years older, showed him an image that opened his world to something he had never seen before. It took only seconds for Bruce to view this image and for his brain to be hooked, and he was haunted for years afterward.

This fleeting look fueled a desire to see more images and more videos, and slowly this brief encounter turned into an addiction. Bruce wrestled with his intense desire and with his determination to keep it a secret, especially from his parents.

A few years later, Bruce found himself in a youth group. It was the first time he heard about honoring God with his eyes and the things he looked at. An overwhelming sense of guilt and shame came over him, and even though he was in a room full of people, he wanted to hide.

There's no doubt about it, pornography cheapens intimacy in relationships. It stunts our emotional growth and hinders us from experiencing true intimacy with God. Study after study shows that both men and women in the church are paralyzed by this addiction. And yet we are sexual beings. The physical response inside us is created by God and intended for good.

Bruce began wrestling with God. Why had God allowed him to see this image so many years ago, and why had it never left him? How would he overcome this addiction? Would he ever be able to see a woman as a person without imagining her with her clothes off? Would he be able to have healthy relationships with women without treating them as objects of his affection?

Bruce confessed this sin to the youth pastor, only to find out that his youth pastor had struggled with looking at images years before. This youth pastor shared that it had been four years since he last looked at pornography and encouraged Bruce that the same could be true for him! Bruce was full of hope that this struggle didn't have to name him "Dirty" or "Ashamed" and that he could fight to become new.

When I met Bruce and his wife years later as adults, he had wrestled with God and fought to become forgiven and new. Bruce's new name was "Forgiven." He was forgiven for looking at the images and objectifying women. God gifted him with a spouse who loved him. He didn't become perfect, but he is forgiven, and he continues to fight for purity with his eyes and in his marriage.

Bruce's new name puts God on display, not his sin. And Bruce's wife, full of grace and mercy, helps us see God's gracious, loving face shining on us as we seek to live into our new names.

Wrestle until you hear the name God calls you. Don't settle for a life of impurity and sin. You will need to confess who you have been and where you're at. But don't expect to stay there. If you want God to give you a new name, He will! God puts each of us in a position to be made new, and He will provide a way out of temptation (1 Corinthians 10:13). God loves when our new name puts Him on display rather than our sin.

WRESTLING FORWARD

Joel and I made the tough decision not to attend my father's funeral. The very next week, I headed to the Social Security office and began the mounds of paperwork necessary to change my legal last name from Fleece to Allen. I wasn't sure I was ready to let go of my maiden name of Fleece, and this surprised me. Though this name held a lot of painful memories, there were also sweet memories. It was familiar, and so much of my life had been shaped—for better and for worse—by this name I had carried to that point. Our old names can become a source of security for us, and they can be hard to let go of.

You may not have mounds of paperwork to file for a name change, but you may have some serious internal work to do—maybe some wrestling with God to discover what your new name is. While it may be easier to live out of our old names, we can miss the beauty, mystery, and challenge that come with pursuing new things in God.

To move from wrestling to acceptance of our new name, we must think of our new name and make a decision. I considered my new last name of Allen. I thought about my husband and how he diligently tried to keep a good name and reputation throughout his high school years, his time at Texas A&M University, and his military career. I thought of his family that has for generations served and followed the one true God.

To be sure, leaving our old names behind may be hard, but there will be times in our faith when God calls us forward, and this was one of those times for me. Many times we can get nostalgic about the things of the past. And while there is often good to be found in our past, we must look forward and decide which name we are going to live out of.

What past is God asking you to trade in? What new name is God calling you to live out of?

Did you see yourself as "not measuring up," and now it's time to believe you have all you need in God? Were you always striving to perform for God's attention, and now you can be known by His affection? Were you once scared to share your faith, and now you have courage to share with others what God has done inside you?

How can you focus on the new thing God has done inside you? Where has your wrestling taken you? It's not prideful to thank God for His new work in you. God celebrates our transformation, and we should too.

STOP STRADDLING THE FENCE

The Old Testament tells of a wicked king named Ahab, who "did more evil in the eyes of the LORD than any of those before him" (1 Kings 16:30). Ahab worshiped false gods and led his country to do the same.

God sent the prophet Elijah to confront the people for their sin of idolatry. In 1 Kings 18:21, Elijah asks the people, "How long will you waver between two opinions? If the LORD is God, follow him; but if Baal is God, follow him."

In a similar way, God may be asking us, "How long will you waver between two names? Will we be known by the ungodly way we used to live or by our new name, and with it our new obedience? Will we be known by our sins of the past? Or will we seek God, persevere through the wrestling, and fight to believe we are forgiven and made new as we anticipate a bright future only He can give?

And how did the Israelites respond? "But the people said nothing" (1 Kings 18:21).

Can you imagine God speaking to you today, asking you one of His signature questions, and you say *nothing*? As God speaks to us, He reveals His heart to transform us. Our silence reveals our backseat ambivalence about allowing such transformation to take place. The absurdity of saying nothing in the face of this astonishing invitation speaks for itself.

Maybe we have trouble hearing from God in the first place. Maybe we don't take the time to hear God and listen for our new name. Maybe we don't believe God has new names for us. Maybe we're comfortable in the same old patterns of identity and action we've known for so long.

The people during Ahab's time straddled the fence and wavered between two identities. Yet today, you and I do not need to waver. We cannot be new creations and live out of our old names—these two things cannot coexist. When we hear our new name, we are tasked with believing and becoming who God says we are.

Just as legally changing one's name is a long and tedious process, a spiritual name change can be a long process too. We have to give ourselves permission to take time and not expect that our new name is going to come easily or without a fight. Some of us will fight for purity with our eyes for the rest of our lives. Some of us will attend codependency meetings for the rest of our lives.

New does not mean "instant" or "overnight." *New* means "not like we used to be." *New* means believing what God says about us and living into this new identity and reality with complete trust in Him. So do what it takes to be new and to stay new. Your old name no longer defines you. Your wrestling has been hard and long, but you have a new identity to show for it.

DON'T GIVE UP IN THE MIDDLE OF A NAME CHANGE!

Jacob's wrestling match and name change marked a new beginning for him. Later in Genesis, Jacob displays humility, forgiveness, and reconciliation with his brother Esau.

Some theologians call Jacob's new name his covenant name, showing how we are bound to an unconditionally loving, covenant-keeping God. Jesus Christ came from Jacob's bloodline; the Messiah came through the nation of Israel. Our new names point to so much more than just us!

In your own dark night of the soul, what question is God asking you? Are you willing to admit the truth? Do you admit to God where you're really at in life, not where you want to be? Can you tell God which label you're listening to and have taken on as your identity? Can you tell God which label you must leave behind?

Another way to look at Jacob's new name, Israel, is to see it as "God strives" (Genesis 32:28). When God gives us a new name, it is because of Christ's work for us on the cross. We are able to "cease striving" (Psalm 46:10 NASB), and so this new name bears witness to what God has done in our lives. Our labels are our old names and our sins, but our new names put God's transforming name and power on display.

As believers, we should never be so ingrained in our old names and ways that we hold on to them forever. Many times, our old names are attached to our old identities, our past mistakes, our external identifiers, and our sins. Old dogs can and should learn new tricks, and old and young people should too. Becoming new is a process we will have to contend for. Discovering our new name does not come easily, and neither does living out of our new name. But this process of transformation and sanctification is worth it.

In other words, the wrestling continues, but it will be worth it.

NAMING THE NEXT GENERATION

Do you believe that God wants a fresh start for you even more than you do? God is kinder than we think He is! We don't have to settle for what our old names meant or how we lived out of them. Ask God today for a new name and wrestle with Him until you hear it. He'd rather have us wrestle in faith than not respond at all.

Jacob married a woman named Rachel. Together they became the parents of two boys named Joseph and Benjamin. Rachel desired children so much that she said in Genesis 30:1, "Give me children, or I'll die!" I recommend approaching God with confidence but holding the way He answers more loosely than Rachel did!

Shortly after Benjamin was born, Rachel named her son Ben-Oni, which means "son of my trouble" (Genesis 35:18). But Jacob, knowing firsthand the importance of naming and the ability to be renamed, changed his name to Benjamin, meaning "son of my right hand."

We need to be careful what we name ourselves, our children, our offenders, and future generations! Naming has power. Our words carry the power of life and death (Proverbs 18:21), and our children are listening!

God will give us a new name, as well as the strength and endurance to live out of our new name. Will we be like the son Ben-Oni and pass on our trouble to the next generation? I surely hope not. Instead, we can look up to our heavenly Father and let

Him rename us. We no longer need to waver between two names. We can listen for our new name and believe God for what we are called. Our new names will not end with us; rather, it begins with us. Future generations will be changed by whether or not we live as new creations.

Some of us will need to get a little grit in our walks with God. We've been hanging on to some of these old names and labels for decades. Even labels that lie can become excusable if we're unwilling to see the effects they have on our souls. While our new names can be mentioned in an instant, it will take a lifetime to learn how to live out of our new identity in Christ. In this process, God is worthy of our self-examination and of our pursuit of Him.

For Further Reflection

Reflection: What can you wrestle with God about? What does wrestling with faith look like? What is the difference between doubt and unbelief?

Prayer of Lament: Lord, for many of my days I've felt like I'm in a wrestling match with You. Why the struggle? How long will the pain go on? Where have You been? Why has the world around me been unkind, and the waters deep? Call me Yours, and provide a way out of temptation. Help me to consider these trials as joy, knowing that You will meet me in them. In Jesus' name I pray. Amen.

Verses to Believe: Romans 8:28; 1 Corinthians 10:13; 1 Peter 5:10

Labels That Limit

Circle which of the old labels you have believed about yourself.

Addicted	Doubter
Afraid/Scared/Anxious	Drunk
Angry	Guilty
Ashamed	Hidden
Cheater	Hypocrite
Coward	Impure
Critic	Judgmental
Crude	Lacking Joy
Deceiver	Mistake
Dirty	Not Measuring Up

Performer	Tired
Porn-Addicted	Unadoptable
Resentful	Unbelieving
Shameful	Unforgiving
Sinner/Stuck in Sin	Ungodly
Skeptic	Unnamed
Struggler	Unwanted
Tempted	Weak in Faith

Your New Name

Circle which of the new names you want to live out of.

Adopted	One Who Moves Forward
Bride	in Faith
Chosen	One Who Overcomes
Courageous	One Who Perseveres
Forgiven	Provided For
Gracious	Pure
Hopeful	Seen by God
Loved by God	Sharer of Faith

PART 2

When God Renames You

CHAPTER 6

Your New Names Are Given and Not Earned

> *"You will leave your name*
> *for my chosen ones to use in their curses;*
> *the Sovereign LORD will put you to death,*
> *but to his servants he will give another name."*
>
> ISAIAH 65:15

I was getting ready to go on a date with Joel, straightening my head full of curly hair, only to walk outside into a torrential downpour. Any curly-haired girl knows straight hair lasts only about one second once the rain or humidity comes. This day had both, and I tried to not let it bother me as we jumped into his white pickup truck to head to dinner.

Joel surprised me by taking me to a place on the lake. Having grown up in Michigan, I love lakes and being on the water, and this helped cheer me up as I was really struggling with the muggy Southern heat.

As the rain came to an end, we saw the most gorgeous sunset unfold. The break in the clouds gave us the perfect opportunity to go for a walk, and to my surprise, Joel got down on one knee and proposed. Without hesitation I shouted out, "Yes!" We hugged each other and celebrated, and a beautiful rainbow filled the sky. It took three full days to let the name "Bride" sink in. I had been in more than a dozen weddings, attended many more than that, and couldn't believe it was going to be my turn to walk down the aisle as a bride.

I had never felt this loved before. I had never felt this chosen. Yet in quiet moments and when I was alone, I battled the same old labels that lied, telling me I was not worth loving to begin with.

PREPARING TO LIVE OUT OF YOUR NEW NAME

The weekend following our engagement, one of my families came to town to visit—the Meyerand family, with whom I lived as I was completing my senior year of high school. We had a full day of touring my fiancé's hometown and introducing our families to one another. Their presence was so meaningful during our engagement bliss.

My sister Cindy Meyerand planned a day full of bridal appointments, and I was bracing myself for the possibility that wedding dress shopping might feel a little bit like bathing suit shopping—dreadful. I expected to be insecure about the extra pounds I wanted to lose and was nervous about how I would afford a dress after just paying my tuition fees at Oxford.

The morning of our appointment, Joel called me. As soon as I answered the phone, he said, "How is my beautiful bride today?" The name "Bride" kept catching me off guard, and knowing I was nervous, Joel told me to imagine God putting the wedding dresses on me.

There was a commotion in the lobby of Neiman Marcus, and a

swarm of dressing room attendants had gathered around someone who appeared to be very important. We snuck past her and went into the dressing room. Honestly, I was trying to go unnoticed. I felt like I didn't deserve to be there, and I certainly didn't want anyone to label me as "broke," unable to pay for these designer gowns. We were there to have fun and let this "Bride" name sink in. No way did I ever think we would leave that store with a dress.

Once I got into the dressing room, I did a quick Google search to find out that the woman causing the commotion was Romona Keveza, one of the most renowned dress designers in the world. Ms. Keveza was there for a trunk show that showcased her wedding dresses. She has made dresses for well-known women around the world, including Michelle Obama, Jennifer Lopez, and Kendall Jenner.

I heard a knock on the dressing room door. There stood Romona. She said she could tell I was the bride-to-be and asked if I'd be willing to try on some of her dresses. It was like other people could see me being a bride even before I could.

She must think I'm somebody else, I thought.

The first wedding gown I tried on was one made for a literal princess. It was the most beautiful garment I had ever laid eyes on. It had delicate fabric with bold, glamorous beads and layered textures of lace that made it an amazement to the human eye. Romona told me the dress took an entire year to make, and I was the first woman in the world to try it on. The dress hugged my curves during a true Cinderella moment.

I have always loved clothes and fashion, and to have a leading dress designer pin this dress to fit me perfectly, find a veil, and help me into designer heels felt like a dream come true. For a moment I thought of selling all my possessions to be able to afford this gown. *Forget the food at the wedding*, my sister and I joked. *I'd be happy to have all of us skip dinner if it could free up the budget for this dress!* The dress made me feel like a million bucks, and for this girl who never felt lovely or pretty, it felt like a price worth paying.

Tears filled my eyes as I looked in the mirror and saw myself as a bride for the first time. Sometimes even when we are called things and people see it for us, we struggle seeing it for ourselves. Have people ever spoke something again and again to you, and you've just brushed them aside or shrugged your shoulders? There in the fitting area, it felt like my whole world stopped and God was getting my attention. Romona's flurry of shop attendants surrounded *me*, and Romona walked over and whispered in my ear, "This is God whispering to you, 'You are beautiful.'"

YOU ARE THE BRIDE OF CHRIST

We don't have to be married to be referred to as a bride of Christ. As God's people, we are to make ourselves ready for Jesus' return, just as a bride makes herself ready for her wedding day (Revelation 19:7–9). The new Jerusalem is also being prepared as a bride adorned for her husband (21:2). Revelation calls the church Jesus' bride (21:9), and Isaiah 54:5 says that our Maker is our husband. Wedding, marriage, and bridal imagery and language are common in Scripture. It's tempting to brush these verses aside when we've been hurt by marriage or haven't seen great examples, but our heavenly marriage won't wound us.

In the same way a young man rejoices over marrying a young woman, God rejoices over us (Isaiah 62:5). When we are in Christ, God considers us His beloved, and this is a beautiful new name we receive.

But here I was, remembering Joel's words to me that morning, listening to Romona and seeing a pattern of my new name coming up again and again. I was a bride, and this name fit me.

As beautiful as this dress was, it was certainly out of my price range. I went back to the dressing room thinking, *Well, that was a moment I'll never forget*, but also feeling a little disappointed that this was better than I deserved. Just then, Romona knocked on the dressing room door again, holding another one of her dresses.

I still didn't feel worthy, and part of me wanted to leave. I didn't feel pretty enough or skinny enough to be trying on these dresses. I unzipped the bag and saw the most beautiful color I had ever seen.

Pink has always been my favorite color, and this dress was a faint blush tone. *How did Romona know I liked pink? Did she know this dress would pull out the golden highlights in my hair?* I put on the dress, and it felt too good to be true. But just because I felt good didn't mean other people would see what I was seeing. We all get hesitant as we learn to live out of our new names.

This dress, though unexpected, gave delicate attention to my curves and brought out the best in me. As soon as I walked out, her team exclaimed, "This one is it!" Romona helped me step up onto a stool to view the full gown and told me she had made this dress with me in mind.

With me in mind? We just met!

Romona and her team affirmed that my frame was perfect for this dress. It was like God Himself was saying that my frame was not hidden from Him when He made me. The words of Psalm 139 rang in my ears. I had never really believed them before, but I was beginning to see these words come to life: "For you created my inmost being; you knit me together in my mother's womb. I praise you because I am fearfully and wonderfully made" (Psalm 139:13–14).

God knew me before I was born. God did not make a mistake when He made me. Just as I had done nothing to earn being called God's bride, or Joel's, I had done nothing to deserve to be God's daughter. I was His because of Him, not because of any effort on my part. I was simply believing God for what He said about me— that I was made by God, that I am loved, and that I was chosen to be His bride: "My frame was not hidden from you when I was made in the secret place, when I was woven together in the depths of the earth" (Psalm 139:15).

I felt God's eyes on me, and I wanted to believe Him. In that moment, I *chose* to believe Him. I no longer wanted to call myself unlovely and unworthy when He called me beautiful. God was using a woman I had just met to affirm that my life was not a mistake and that I could be named "Beautiful Bride." We can miss God's best gifts and names for us when they are unexpected and look different from the way we expected them to look.

The Meyerands could see how much I loved the beautiful blush dress. As we walked back to the dressing room, Mom Meyerand said that she and Dad Meyerand wanted to gift my wedding dress to me. Tears flooded my eyes as God not only affirmed my name and frame, but provided me with a gift I could not afford. I had skipped high school dances growing up because I could not afford a dress, and here I would have a wedding dress fit for a queen. It was such a beautiful picture of the way God chooses us, names us, and blesses us out of His abundant goodness.

Romona's assistant Blake immediately got on the phone to rush-order the dress. They added extra details like buttons in the back to make the wedding gown uniquely me—at no additional charge. This would be the first dress of its kind in the blush tone, and I couldn't help but physically blush during what would become one of the most beautiful days of my life.

Romona pulled out a *Bridal* magazine in which one of her dresses was featured in an ad in the magazine's centerfold and signed a note to me: "To Esther, a legendary bride in your own time. XO Romona." It was a day I will never forget.

God doesn't just gift us by meeting our needs; He provides new names more beautiful than we could ever imagine. He called me a bride in a spiritual sense and was making a way for me to become a physical bride here on earth too. In the same way, God's names for you are better than you could ask for or imagine. God loves giving us new names and new beginnings. He is in the business of making us new!

HOW TO BELIEVE GOD

The enemy of your soul will never encourage you or speak life into who you are. The enemy will never affirm who you are becoming; instead, he tries to distract you or make you think your new name is earned and not given. The truth is, none of us can live "good enough" to earn a new name from God. God names us because of who He is and out of His love! When we hear painful lies from our past or when our old names or identities resurface, we need to ask, "Who is speaking this name over me?"

I used to hear things like, "You will never be married." "No one will ever want you." "You are not desirable." And if we pause to think about these statements, we realize they are accusations. "*You* this, *you* that." We wouldn't look at ourselves in the mirror and talk like this to ourselves. When we hear dreadful accusations in the name-changing process, we can be sure it is the enemy and not God, trying to proclaim identities over us that have *never* been true.

So how can we discern the difference between these voices?

God's voice is gentle and kind. God's voice provides guidance. Even when God corrects us, He does so out of love (Hebrews 12:6). God's kindness leads us to repentance (Romans 2:4), and God's words will always match Scripture. God's words are full of truth and show an everlasting kindness toward us (Jeremiah 31:3). God's words sound like:

- You matter to someone (Psalm 139:17).
- You are not a mistake (Ephesians 4:1).
- You are loved (Psalm 86:5).

God's words are affirming and loving, even when He is correcting us. When we hear accusations directed at us, there's a good chance the accusation is trying to take the place of our new name.

Don't let it! Don't believe the lie that "you are not enough," and ask God to help you hear His voice of truth.

When I heard the words "You are not loved," they led me to isolation and could have prevented me from giving my heart to Joel. But when we listen to God, the Holy Spirit will "guide us into all the truth" (John 16:13). The Holy Spirit will tell us our new name by affirming us, not by putting us down. The Holy Spirit will never shame us into believing God. The Holy Spirit will never lie to us, mock us, or attack us. The Holy Spirit reminds us of who God has already made us to be—His own.

When life is hard, sometimes our old names and identities resurface. As wedding planning became stressful and bills piled up, it was easy for me to believe my name was "Poor" or "Undeserving." But these were accusations. They evoked the old labels and not the new names God had given me. And slowly I began to learn to challenge them, clinging to what God says about me instead.

God was my provider. Not only did God provide a godly husband, but He was delighted in our covenant marriage. God wanted to speak words of life, love, and affirmation over my wedding day. Any voice of guilt or shame was a distraction that tried to get my eyes off my new name.

I am not poor; I am provided for. I am not unworthy; I am lovely. I am not orphaned; I am chosen, and you are too.

The true words God speaks about us have the power to extinguish any influence our old labels may have once had.

RETRAINING YOUR MIND

On a regular basis, I ask God to help me renew my mind (Romans 12:2) and help me believe what He says about me. Ask God to help you hear for yourself how He sees you. Tell God you need a reminder of who you are and who you belong to. It's as easy as praying, "God, I am believing this about me, but how do You see me? Or praying, "God, I am hearing this lie about who I am. Who do You say I am?" And after you ask, look for ways He may be speaking to you. It may be through His Word, someone you know, or a complete stranger, like a celebrity wedding dress designer. But God wants to speak beautiful names over you—names better than you can see for yourself—and He will go to great lengths to do so!

And when you hear your new name, write it down. After I heard the name "Bride" from both Joel and God, I went out and bought a key chain with the word *Bride* on it. I needed to remind myself what God said. We must take an active role in believing and living into our new names. Just as I had to make wedding preparations, I had to make emotional and spiritual preparations for living up to my name. We are so prone to get busy and to forget the names God has spoken over us. So do your part to write it down to help yourself remember the beautiful and true things God has spoken over you.

OLD NAMES AND OLD COPING MECHANISMS

It's fun to tell some of my new stories—like becoming a bride, for example—but things weren't always this new and beautiful. When I was in ninth grade, I spent one evening alone in the hospital, recovering from a suicide attempt. I had just gotten into a horrible physical fight with my mother. She removed me from the cheerleading team out of her misplaced anger, and I was taking all the abandonments and physical abuses personally, figuring the world would be better off without me in it.

I don't know who told a local youth pastor I was there, but he came to visit me in the hospital. Even though I had only visited his youth group a few times, I was recently awarded the monthly prize in that youth group—a gift card to Starbucks—for bringing the most friends with me to church. It was a stark contrast—losing my will to live while being popular and having a lot of friends. And it's why this pastor was surprised to find me in the suicide ward of a local psychiatric hospital. There was so much going on in my life at the time—my father going to jail, my stepfather leaving us, my mother neglecting me. I remember getting the idea when a friend in school took his life by suicide. It was the first time the enemy accused me with such destructive lies like "Your life isn't worth living" and "Things will never get better."

I didn't have what it took to live into the new identity that was already mine. I needed God's true word spoken over my life—in God's power and not in my own.

I never thought suicide was a good idea; I just thought it was my only way to end life as I knew it. I felt like the people I cared about the most had abandoned me, and I was waiting for God to leave me too. I heard lies like "You deserve this" and "You're alone," and at that time I wasn't familiar with Jesus as "a man of suffering, and familiar with pain" (Isaiah 53:3). I had yet to learn about Jesus' tears or how one of Jesus' closest friends betrayed Him. I wish I'd known then that crying can sometimes be the healthiest response to emotional pain.

The pastor who showed up, only in his twenties but with a deep love for and knowledge of God, said, "Esther, you are the last person I would expect to take your life. You have so much going for you. Why do you want to do this?"

He saw the awards and the recognition, and he heard my laughter and saw my smile. But my outsides had fooled many people about what was inside. I replied, "Everyone in my life who loves me leaves me. I'm sure that God is the next to leave. Somehow even when people assure me, 'God loves you,' those words stir up fear in my unsettled heart." I was allowing the old labels like "unwanted" and "forgotten" to stick.

I would have preferred to have my life end than to suffer the pain of being abandoned by God. The "do not be anxious about anything" Bible verse (Philippians 4:6) on the front of my new journal just wasn't helping. It's easy for people to encourage us to pray anxiety away when they've never experienced anxiety themselves.

All of us have something that feels worse than death. What is the one thing you think you could not make it through? Maybe it's a divorce, or maybe it's the death of a child. Some of us fear unemployment or news of a betrayal. Or maybe there are dreams and desires you don't think you can live without—like the dream of being married or the desire to have a baby.

For me, the thing worse than death was abandonment. After being cut off from my biological family, I felt defeated and unable to go on. Whenever this pain resurfaced, I was triggered to go back to my old coping mechanisms. The pain made room for the enemy to remind me of the old labels that denied the new names God had given me: "Daughter," "Loved," "Chosen."

ATTACKS COME AS GOD CHANGES US

Two decades after my unsuccessful suicide attempt, and just six months into our marriage, Joel and I came home to a certified letter from a law office in Florida.

My heart sank, and I imagined this had something to do with my father because of the Florida mailing address. The first thing that came to mind was that he was in some legal trouble that I was going to need to sort out and finalize. Part of my father's mental illness revealed itself in his habit of filing lawsuits over petty and frivolous things. *How is my father still wounding me?* I thought to myself.

We opened the letter, and the headline read, in large caps,

"HOMEOWNERS ASSOCIATION SUING ESTHER M. FLEECE." I could barely breathe as I kept reading. The lawsuit was directed at heirs of my father for unpaid homeowners association fees of more than $12,000—a steep fee for failing to pay for the mowing of the grass in front of a low-income condo building. The homeowners association filed a suit, giving me just twenty days to respond.

How was my new life with my new name disrupted again? Why couldn't my past stay in the past? How would we fight this as a newly married couple struggling to pay our bills?

Even after we receive our new names, the enemy will come knocking at our door to attempt to convince us that we're not really new. Sometimes he deceives us in subtle ways, and sometimes he overplays his cards. Even living as Esther Allen, I sometimes had to deal with my old name.

I felt like my father was taking advantage of me all over again, and I doubted God's protection. My father was deceased, yet he was still causing me pain. He had left me decades before, yet he still had the ability to wound me deeply. A friend of mine called this "pains from the grave," and my emotional response was to feel trapped by my old feelings of being an unloved daughter. I was forgetting to live out of my new name.

I loved my new life, my new name, and my husband, but those old familiar feelings of wanting to die crept back in. This pain went so deep, triggering memories of my abandonment by that entire side of the family, that suicidal thoughts again entered my mind. My despair felt wild and spiraling, even in the midst of this beautiful life I was now living. I just couldn't reconcile this pain with my current circumstances. I was deeply in love with God, yet deeply distressed at the suffering brought about by this lawsuit, as well as at other betrayals and difficulties going on during this time. Seeing my father's name again was pulling me back to a reality I had fought so hard to break free from.

When God speaks a new name over us, we can expect an attack from the enemy to be right around the corner. There was no way a homeowners association should sue an estranged child for thousands of dollars when their father dies. In a similar way, the enemy throws things at you with the goal of stealing your focus on your new name, lying to you about your old name, or taking you out altogether. Maybe an old relationship resurfaces that sets you off track, or a job loss causes you to doubt yourself and God. Be on the lookout for something or someone trying to get you off track and cause you to lose sight of what God has recently done inside you. This is why it's helpful to write down our new names. We need to fight to believe them as we become them.

During this time, I was battling again with the label "fatherless." My emotions went haywire as I felt shame from my past and my maiden name, Fleece. My excitement as a new bride faded as I was plagued with anxiety about how this lawsuit might unfold. How would it affect my marriage? How would we respond to the court?

This time I did not really want to die. I was truly very happily married; I just didn't want to live through the family pain yet again. Sometimes our pain is too deep for words, and we would do anything to escape it. I need to be honest with you. Receiving a new identity may be the hardest work we'll ever do on earth. Sometimes it can be easier to live out of our old names or ignore self-reflection altogether. But there is a steep price to pay for avoidance. Not only does it limit our relationship with God, but it also hinders our relationships with others and can cause us to miss out on hearing our new names altogether.

Old labels triggered old lies. *Will I always be unwanted? Will life always be this hard? Why doesn't my new name protect me from the attacks of the enemy? Why doesn't my new life allow me to escape old pains?* Be on guard when your old coping mechanisms come back and make themselves look attractive. Don't give in to them, but in faith ask God to help you withstand.

A GOD WHO SAVES US
AGAIN AND AGAIN

Maybe you're not tempted by suicidal and self-harm thoughts. Maybe your temptation is self-doubt, isolation, or substance abuse to numb the pain. We all have unhealthy coping mechanisms and go-to habits that come with the old labels we once wore. The challenge in the name-changing process is to find new ways to cope, new ways to pray, and new ways to live healthier out of our new names.

I needed a fresh reminder of permission to pray and to lament, even after decades of following God. God is okay with this. In fact, our tears can often be the oil that helps to remove those old, sticky labels, preparing our hearts to receive the new name God has for us. He knows we need reminders of who we really are, and He puts people in our lives to gently nudge us back to the truth about Him. Joel has been one of those persons in my life. And during that season of anxiety over the lawsuit, I needed a reminder that God would parent me through this trial, just as He had done in every trial leading up to this one.

When I was saved by God as a child, I was completely reidentified and renamed as God's child. I was taught that you only have to say the "salvation prayer" once and you become a Christian.

Lord, I know I am a sinner. I ask for Your forgiveness. I believe Jesus Christ is the Son of God who died for my sins. I believe He rose from the dead to give me eternal life. I want to follow Him as Lord. Forgive my sins and help me live for You. Amen.

But God is *still* saving us! While we only need to ask God into our hearts once for our eternal salvation, "save me" is a very common prayer for those of us who are already saved. The lie we're tempted to believe is that after God saves our souls once, we're on our own to buckle down, live right, and run our own lives. The lie is that we don't *still* need God to save us because we can somehow manage to live into our new identities on our own.

Except we can't. We still need God to save us. To name us. To reidentify us.

When Paul writes in Romans 10:9, "If you declare with your mouth, 'Jesus is Lord,' and believe in your heart that God raised him from the dead, you will be saved." *Saved (klaio* in Greek) means to be rescued and delivered from the power of sin and death.

The "save me" prayer also appears in other forms. The psalmist cried out, "Save me, for I am yours; I have sought out your precepts" (Psalm 119:94). This "save me" (*yasha* in Hebrew) is used in the prayers of believers when they ask to be helped, to persevere, to be saved from adversaries, to be protected from violence, and more. This "save me" prayer is what I can pray to be saved from evil threats (Psalm 57:3) and even from my ongoing fears (Psalm 34:4).

When I received that notice about the lawsuit, I needed a "save me" prayer again!

We call on the *name* of the Lord to be saved (Romans 10:13), and our sins are forgiven because of the *name* of Jesus (1 John 2:12). Have you ever wondered why the word *name* appears in these Scriptures? Why aren't we just saved? Why are we saved in the *name* of the Lord? We are in constant need of the name of the Lord, and He will go to great lengths to speak to us our new name.

Throughout the renaming process, I want to give you permission to call out to God's name, asking for His help and crying out in prayer, "Save me." Some of us have been delivered from hell, but we fail to ask God to continue to save us and help us live out of our new names. Some of us prayed the salvation prayer once as a child, but we fail to cry out, "Save me!" for spiritual and emotional health. When we pray, "Save me," we affirm God's sovereignty and power to deliver us and heal us completely, and we humbly acknowledge that God is the One who gives us a new identity and makes us whole. When we stop praying, "Save me," we get confident in our own abilities to save ourselves.

We hear "save me" prayers throughout the book of Psalms. David, a man known by God and loved by God, asks God to save him: "Save me from the guilt of bloodshed, God—God of my salvation" (Psalm 51:14 CSB). Just a few chapters later, David writes:

> As for me, I call to God,
>   and the LORD saves me.
> Evening, morning and noon
>   I cry out in distress,
>   and he hears my voice.
>
> PSALM 55:16–17

Why did David pray these things if he was already a follower of God? Why did David ask God to save him if he was already saved? Because one of God's names is "the God who saves me" (Psalm 88:1), and David called out to a God who saves us over and over again. God never tires of hearing His children ask Him to save.

We can pray "save me" as we cry out to God for our new names. Since you have become His, have you asked Him to save you in other ways? Have you asked God to save you from emotional distress? Maybe your old name is "Anxious," and God wants to give you the new name "Peace" or "Calm." Or maybe your name is "Depressed," and He wants to put His spirit of joy inside you instead of despair. We can ask God to save us and remind us of the names that are most true about who we really are. Asking God for His help in our name-changing process is key to hearing from Him and receiving His help again and again.

It is God Himself who keeps us in His love and faith, not our words or actions or circumstances. Keeping the faith is not solely on us. Neither is living out of our new names. We need God's help to believe and become who He says we are.

My wedding dress was given to me as a gift. I received it through no effort of my own. In the same way, God wants to give you a new name to empower you to live a Christian life. And that's exactly what our new names do! They set us free from the labels slapped on us by the one who lies, and they empower us to be who we really are—God's beloved.

For Further Reflection

Reflection: Do you believe God has good gifts for you? What do you know and believe about the character of God? Do you believe God is for you? What can you ask Him for?

Prayer of Petition: Thank You, Lord, that You do not withhold good from those who walk uprightly. Help me to walk uprightly. If You did not spare Your own Son but gave Him up for me, how will You not, along with Him, graciously give me all things? Thank You that You are for me. Please call me a name based on who You are and not on what I've done. Thank You for giving good gifts to Your children. Help me to receive all that You have for me, because Your name, Jesus, has the power to save. Amen.

Verses to Believe: Romans 8:32; James 1:17

Labels That Limit
Circle which of the old labels you have believed about yourself.

Alone	Not Pretty
Broken	Poor
Disappointment	Undeserving
Fatherless	Undesirable/Unlovely
Forever Alone	Unloved
Forgotten	Unwanted
Not Enough	Unworthy

Your New Name

Circle which of the new names you want to live out of.

Beautiful

Bride Adorned for Her Husband

Chosen

Daughter

Jesus' Bride

Known by God

Loved

One Made on Purpose

One Who Matters

Peaceful

Sacred

Wife/Husband

Wonderfully Made

Yours

CHAPTER 7

Your New Names Are Better Than You Can See for Yourself

"See, the former things have taken place,
and new things I declare;
before they spring into being
I announce them to you."
ISAIAH 42:9

When I was a little girl, I had a doll house that I would play with every day. I don't remember who bought it for me, but I remember it was full of Barbie dolls and their accessories. I dressed my dolls, played with their hair, and carried them around with me everywhere I went. Each of them had a name too. I loved naming them. Like any child fixated on their favorite toy, I would play with these dolls for hours. I was their mother, their teacher, and their personal stylist.

As I got older I became a babysitter. I was the first person in the fifth grade to sign up for a babysitter training class. I became certified by sixth grade and became a mother's helper. I babysat and even nannied for a family with four young boys while still in elementary school.

As the years went on, my life was surrounded with children. When I was kicked out of my home in high school, God provided a live-in nannying job for me for a family with five children. This family played a significant role in teaching me the blessing of children. I have deep joy in my heart whenever I'm around my Elliss family members, and I consider each of these children to be my siblings.

If you were to ask anyone around me as I was growing up, they would describe me as a people-person and a kid-person. People would compliment my playfulness with children and my ability to make children laugh, play, and smile. But I could never see this for myself. Even though my life included children, I didn't think about having children of my own.

Why didn't you think kids were for you? you ask. Well, because of the name "Mom." That name came with so much baggage. We talk about father wounds a lot in the church, but we're largely silent about mother wounds, and mine were severe.

I DON'T WANT *THAT* NAME

The name "Mom" carried so much hurt for me that I never wanted to take on that name myself. In my early years, I remember loving my mother, but as time went on and life hurt us again and again, our relationship broke.

I know I'm not alone in this. Scripture even says your mother may abandon you, but the Lord will not forget you (Isaiah 49:15). I have a few good friends who chose not to have children because of the fear of becoming like their mom. When names scare us, they keep us from receiving some of God's gifts in our lives.

Before I go on, let me say that there are *so* many good moms out there—good married moms, good single moms, good moms in training, and good spiritual moms. We need to celebrate moms every day and value the role they fill in our homes, our society, and our world. "Mom" is a beautiful name, and it is a gloriously beautiful, hard job. Moms work in our schools, homes, and churches, and they are valuable for what they do and who they are—and being a mom is not their only role or identity! But how do you interact with that name? What does it stir up inside you?

For some single women, the name "Mom" can call to mind an emptiness. It may be a name they hope to have someday. To a mom grieving the death of a child, the name "Mom" reminds them of their painful loss. To a woman struggling with infertility, the name "Mom" triggers questions about what she will become.

See how the same name can awaken different emotions in each of us?

The name "Mom" can stir up emotions in men too. Ask several men what this name means to them, and you'll get vastly different answers. Names have nuances. I think we can all admit that the name "Mom" is a beautiful one; it's just a name I never thought was for me.

WHAT DO YOU SEE IN YOURSELF?

Two decades after I played with my dolls, my friend Ryan asked me, "Esther, what did you do as a kid that you loved?"

I thought it was a really good question. I had to pause and think about it. I had experienced so many bad things as a child. What had I done for fun?

While I didn't answer Ryan on the spot, I went home and thought about his question. My answer, reluctantly, was that I enjoyed pretending to be a mom as I was growing up. Some girls dress up as princesses and some boys dress up as superheroes, but I liked playing a mom. My good memories involved playing with dolls and giving them a mom, a dad, and children. How was this once a reality and now a far distant memory? I pretended to be a mom every day with my dolls, and I had forgotten that dream and desire completely. I disregarded the name "Mom" when in my vocabulary the name became identified with scars.

When my mother left me, it was the worst pain I'd experienced to that point. Yes, having my father leave our family was crushing. It caused me to question the presence of God. Yes, having my stepfather leave the family was also devastating. It caused me to question the faithfulness of men. But when my mother left me, it caused me to question my own womanhood—like, how would I become a woman on my own? Who would teach me about women things? If my own mom could hurt me so deeply, I never wanted to be a mom who could risk hurting her children.

All of us have hurts, pains, longings silenced, and longings still to be realized. It helps to know we all have brokenness in our past. This should normalize every one of us and maybe even take away some of the blame from our parents. But even those of us with broken pasts can usually remember a few good things about our past.

At least I hope you can.

What did you enjoy doing when you were a child? Did you play with dolls? Play dress up? Build tree houses? Play with trains? Pretend you could fly? Not all of us will get to do what we loved as a child, but you never know where those first loves might lead. And we risk losing these first loves if they are shut down by others.

I have a friend named Travis who almost shut down his athletic career because a coach told him he'd never be good enough to earn a college scholarship. He went on to play in the National Football League for fourteen years. My husband built tree houses as a child, and now he's a homebuilder. My friend Ryan played with Legos nonstop. Now he is a developer in San Diego, creating workspaces, restaurants, and more with his group, Moniker.

You may not have a bad association with the names "Mom" and

"Dad," but were you ever called a name you wanted to avoid? Were you named "Nerd," and so you tried your hardest to be cool by purchasing the right shoes and clothes? Were you named "Failure" in one area of life, and so you overachieved in another area? Maybe you were named "Poor," and now you're working hard at not being associated with that name by buying things you don't need.

Whether we admit it or not, the names we were called affect us. And we can agree or disagree with a name so strongly that we'll do our best to avoid that name at all costs—even if that name is as beautiful as "Mom." How many of us have shut down careers, callings, and dreams, all because we were afraid to associate with a name?

ABRAM TO ABRAHAM AND
SARAI TO SARAH

Names are important to God, and they were also special and significant within the ancient Jewish culture. The Jewish people would celebrate a baby dedication and circumcision (a sign of the covenant) and name a baby on the same day. All three were important ways to welcome a child into the world, and their name would signify what God would have them become.

There was an Old Testament woman named Sarai, who was outspoken and strong-willed (Genesis 21:8–11) and beautiful (12:11, 14). Sarai was the wife of Abram (11:29), one of the most famous men in the Bible. Abram was a patriarch of the human race, and he received a promise from God that he would be the "father of many nations" (17:4) even before he had a single child: "And in you all the families of the earth shall be blessed" (12:3 NKJV).

Yet even while having the blessing and favor of God and the promise of descendants, Abram and Sarai experienced infertility (Genesis 11:30; Romans 4:19), a great pang of the human heart.

Abram was given a new name by God, and he went from

Abram to Abraham, representing a new beginning. Abraham may mean "father of many," and this came to pass as God fulfilled His promises to Abraham to make him the father of nations (Genesis 17:4). While I'm sure this new name gave Abraham great confidence and courage, I imagine as the years went on and he saw his wife struggle with the pain of a hope deferred, Abraham must have wondered how his legacy would ever extend beyond him.

God had also promised Sarai that she would produce a son (Genesis 17:16), but as she grew in years, this promise felt more and more distant. Many women feel "too old" to have children when they reach their forties and fifties. Imagine Sarah reaching her sixties, seventies, and eighties with no child in sight. Imagine her shrinking hope of a swelling belly as her body began to show signs of age. You can imagine she'd feel God had forgotten His promise to her. Sarai may well have given up on the dream of being named "Mom." Sometimes I wonder what her prayers in these years of waiting looked like.

Finally, Sarai must have felt she'd had enough. She took matters into her own hands and urged Abram to have a child with her slave Hagar (Genesis 16:1–2). It's astounding that a wife would "volunteer" another woman to her husband like this, especially a woman who, as a slave, had no say in the matter.

There was enormous pressure on women to bear children, particularly sons, in that day and age. A woman's identity was often tied up in whether she could bear children. Sarai and her family received a promise from God and they hadn't seen it come to pass, so she took it upon herself to turn this long-lost dream into reality.

What Sarai did may seem incomprehensible, yet if we're honest, how many times do we impatiently wait for God's timing in our own lives? We can all relate to ignoring God's rules and writing our own as we confess to our failed attempts to expedite God's timing by taking matters into our own hands.

Sarai's slave Hagar went on to have a child with Abram. Hagar became the mother of Ishmael (Genesis 16:15), and Sarai's name and promise still looked unachievable. Yet God told Abraham that Sarai's name would change to Sarah and she would bear a son (Genesis 17:15–16). God was announcing that Sarah would be "the mother of nations." Abraham's response was laughter at the thought of Sarah becoming a mom at ninety years old (17:17), but God's plan would not be denied. God renamed Sarai to Sarah and made it possible for her to live out of this new physical and spiritual identity. What grace that God renames us, even when we take matters into our own hands!

God was faithful to the end, fulfilling his promise that Sarah would become a mother of a multitude. Abraham and Sarah became the patriarch and matriarch of the Jewish people—with a lineage that continues to this day! Sarah became a mother of nations, physically and spiritually speaking, in a much bigger way than she ever could have imagined. Sarai wanted one child, and God wanted her lineage to be remembered throughout generations. God's plans are so much more substantial than ours. We just need the patience to see them come into being. God didn't need Sarah's help, nor does He need our help to expedite the process of receiving our new name.

And what about Hagar? She was wronged by those who manipulated their circumstances instead of waiting on God's promises. Her entire life was altered by these choices. Yet God saw her. She did not escape His attention. When Hagar became pregnant, Sarah mistreated her, and Hagar ran away into the desert. An angel of the Lord appeared to Hagar, telling her that the Lord had listened to her in her misery (Genesis 16:7–11). In Hagar's worry and fear, God saw her and took care of her. Hagar became the first person in Scripture to call God "the God who sees me" (16:13). Even when we've been wronged and cast aside by others, God sees us for who we are. He does not get hung up on our labels. He sees us in the whole of our unique identity created just for us.

TRANSFORMATION INTO A NEW IDENTITY

While this name-changing process is deeply personal between us and God, our transformation will not stay private. Sarai wanted one son, while God wanted her to become a mother of nations. God wanted me to become a mother, while I was content to be a babysitter.

Certain names in the Bible, like Abraham and Sarah, are considered sacramental names—names given by God Himself. Herbert Lockyer teaches that these names come under God's inspiration "in association with a particular promise, covenant or declaration of His, as to the character, destiny or mission of those distinctly named."[7] While God may speak to us in different ways today than in Abraham's day, the principle is the same: God births new names inside us.

But we first have to let Him see us in our mess, our sins, our mistreatment of others, and our secrets. Pretending is not an option in the presence of a holy God. But we don't need to pretend. God doesn't always rename us when we are at our best; often God renames us when we are wounded and in desperate need of Him. God isn't expecting your perfection, but He is requiring your honesty. God will not be manipulated, but He is asking permission to see into the very depth of you. Will you give Him that permission?

What name does God have for you? I can guarantee that your new name is bigger and more glorious than the small dream or goal you have for yourself. Can you ask God to help you wait on this new name and not take matters into your own hands and create one yourself?

ADAM NAMED EVE

While God gives names in Scripture, and we find names there that point to who God is, we also have occasion to name someone.

Did you know that Adam named Eve? In Genesis 3:20, we read, "Adam named his wife Eve."

I had always assumed that God named Eve—in the same way that God named Adam. But I was wrong. Adam was given authority by God to name the animals (Genesis 2:20), and because there was no suitable mate for Adam, God made Eve.

The name Adam is related to the Hebrew word for "ground," which points to his origins, just as our names can point to our family of origin. But Adam named his wife Eve for what she would become. Eve would become "the mother of all the living" (Genesis 3:20), but notice the timing of Eve receiving her name. Adam named Eve *before* she bore any children, thereby calling out what she would become.

Sometimes others can see our new name before we can see it for ourselves. And sometimes God names us for what we are to become. Do you have someone in your life who can call out the good, true, and beautiful in you?

My friend Lynette Lewis is a beautiful, smart, hardworking woman of valor. Lynette had always dreamed of becoming a wife and mom, but after attending a Christian university and not meeting the man of her dreams, she moved to New York City and landed on a high-power career path. Lynette never set out to be a career woman, but it seemed to be the story God was writing for her life, so she made the best of it.

Year after year, Lynette felt she was missing out on her prime childbearing years, and as she entered her thirties, forties, and fifties without bearing children, her "why, God?" prayers felt unanswered. Have you ever felt left behind in a season of your life?

After the terrorist attacks happened on 9/11, God sent a church-planting pastor to New York City to start a church. This pastor was a single dad to four boys, and he and Lynette met and fell in love. After all the years of longing for a family, Lynette became a wife and stepmom on the very same day. It wasn't an easy journey from that point on. This couple faced infertility, miscarriage, and delayed adoptions.

Lynette taught me so much in her season of waiting. I learned that even if women can't bear children, women are created to create. Through our vision, we can create with our hands, bodies, and minds. Creating life is not limited to physical procreation. Yes, we can be fruitful biologically, but we can also be fruitful vocationally, artistically, and in ministry. There are many ways to be givers of life.

As Lynette struggled to have a baby, she began creating something new with her mind. She founded the organization Stop Child Trafficking Now and began rescuing children who were caught in human trafficking. Lynette has helped heal physical wounds of women and girls all over the world and has restored many spiritual orphans. What if Lynette would have taken on the name "Infertile," like doctors called her, or "Hopeless" when she felt devastated from a miscarriage? Instead, Lynette created elsewhere. She birthed new things when the door closed to birthing children. Women are created to create, and we can create in a myriad of ways.

There is a great need for spiritually and emotionally healthy women in our culture today, not only physical birth moms. Bearing children, while important, is not the crown of womanhood. How could it be, when our Savior never married or bore physical children of His own? Honoring God in every area is ultimate. Seeking first God's kingdom and righteousness is of the utmost importance (Matthew 6:33). The roles of wife and mother, if God calls us to them, are beautiful callings and lovely names, but they're not ultimate—just as having the right job or making lots of money is not ultimate. We are children of God first, and living out of this new name will help us live fruitful lives, no matter what God calls us into.

FUTURE HOPE

Sarai was called the mother of nations before she had the physical ability to bear children. Abraham was told he would be the father of many nations before he had any children of his own. Eve was a giver of life before she bore children. God's names for us call us forward into God's promises. Notice that it wasn't good deeds and merit that achieved for them their new names. Their new names were given out of God's love for them and His desire to bless the inhabitants of the earth through the gift of Jesus the Messiah.

Just as God saw potential in each of these Bible characters, God sees things in you and will call them out even before you can see them for yourself. God loves you and is for you! He doesn't rename you because He doesn't like the old you; He renames you to make you a closer version of who He's created you to be. Our new names put the emphasis on God's transforming work inside us rather than on our mistakes. Our new names carry on the name of Jesus Christ as we receive our hope and life and newness in Him.

It is crucial to see God's larger story in the process of our name change. God sees things in us and will call them out because He loves us and wants to see His story of love continue.

CALL OUT GOOD THINGS
YOU SEE IN OTHERS

While Joel was stationed at an Air Force base in Washington State, he had a couple take him under their wing. They were his family away from family. They loved him like a son and encouraged him when he first moved away from home. Paul and Tammy Rohrbaugh are the best kind of people—the kind of Christians you wish non-Christians would first encounter, because they're not only cultured and cool but are also so down-to-earth that it's hard not to like them. After hearing about the Rohrbaughs for a year, I surprised Joel by using frequent flyer miles to book a ticket to Seattle to celebrate his birthday and meet this family. I was wondering if I would fit in or be the awkward one left out.

I hit it off with this family and found that they use their words to bless and encourage others. They were much wiser than we were, yet kind enough to ask questions in a way that allowed them to genuinely get to know us. I couldn't help but like this couple and be challenged by them immediately.

Paul and Joel headed off to a men's group where Paul was going to teach on being transformed by God. "Part of the transformation we experience," Paul said, "is that our old nature doesn't fit us anymore." Paul used the example of how he used to be a validation seeker, wanting approval and acceptance from people. But since Christ has changed him, he now encourages people instead of looking for their approval.

Paul and Joel came home from this group and told of how when Paul shared the transformation he went through, other men in the group began to reflect on the ways God had changed them too.

"I think my new name is 'Bold,'" a man named Joe had said. "Before Christ transformed me, I was timid and cowardly. Now I have a confidence to share my faith with others."

More men courageously began to share their stories.

"I was a cheat, and now I'm a collaborator."

"I was angry, and now I'm able to express my feelings in a healthy way."

"I was a compulsive gambler, and now I'm a generous giver."

One by one the men began to tell of their old name, their old story, and their new identity, sharing how they had been made new.

Most of us agree we'd much rather hang out with encouragers, collaborators, and people who are patient than with those who are angry, who cheat, and who are people pleasers. But many times we're tempted to skip over our transformation altogether. Sometimes we forget to remind people of how we've been made new. But isn't this an incredible thought? Our words have power— power to proclaim truth, to prompt transformation, and to lift others into who God has called them to be all along.

Our new names are a gift from God. Our name change is not a transformation story about us; it's a story about God's work inside us that enables us to live differently than we did before. When we are fooled into thinking our transformation story is about us, we are missing the emphasis of the apostle Paul in 2 Corinthians: "And we all, who with unveiled faces contemplate the Lord's glory, are being transformed into his image with ever-increasing glory, which comes from the Lord, who is the Spirit" (2 Corinthians 3:18).

We are transformed, changed, made new, not so we can become just a better version of ourselves, but so we can become more like Christ as those made in His image. And this verse from 2 Corinthians reminds us that our help comes from the Holy Spirit. So if we are not changing and being made new, it may be wise to ask if the Spirit of God is inside us. Where are the stories of old being made new in our churches today?

GOD'S NAME SAVES US

Thankfully for us, God does not disqualify us from receiving a new name based on our record of sin. If He did, Sarai, Abram, David, you, and me would never get a new name; we would all be stuck. Your new name is "Forgiven," because Christ forgives you (Ephesians 4:32) and does not remember your sin (Isaiah 43:25).

Does anybody out there need to take on the new name "Forgiven by God"? If we confess our sins, God forgives us of our sins (1 John 1:9). Dwelling on our past sin and old names fails to put the emphasis on God and how He has made us new.

Our new names call us to a greater level of service, sacrifice, and faithfulness than our old names could handle. It will require faith to lean into our new name even before we fully see it and understand it. If you don't know what your new name is yet, spend some time meditating on what it means to be loved and forgiven by God. Believe that God has a new name for you that is better than what you're settling for. He gives us kids good gifts and names that will be better than we can see for ourselves!

For Further Reflection

Reflection: What have others told you they see in you? Are you hospitable, kind, or giving? How can these affirmations move you to explore the spiritual affirmation that God calls out to you? What do you think God sees inside you? How can you pursue this in a way that honors Him?

Prayer of Listening: Heavenly Father, thank You for seeing things in me that I cannot yet see for myself. Your kingdom is not just talk, but power. Open my eyes to see wonderful things from Your law. I need Your supernatural help to live out of who You say I am. Fill me with Your Holy Spirit and empower me to live boldly and in newness of life. In Jesus' name. Amen.

Verses to Believe: Acts 4:29–31; Ephesians 5:18–20

Labels That Limit
Circle which of the old labels you have believed about yourself.

Angry	Infertile
Broken Past	Nerd
Cheat	Poor
Coward	Stuck in Pain
Failure	Too Old
Gambler	Validation/Approval Seeker
Guilty	Wounded
Hopeless	

Your New Name

Circle which of the new names you want to live out of:

Bold	Forgiven
Builder	Giver
Collaborator	Giver of Life
Communicator	Loved by God
Creator	Mother/Father
Encourager	Seen by God
Fearless	

CHAPTER 8

Your New Names Are Personal

"To the one who is victorious, I will give some of the hidden manna. I will also give that person a white stone with a new name written on it, known only to the one who receives it."

REVELATION 2:17

One of my most compassionate friends struggles with the apostle Paul. She finds his tone to be harsh and insensitive. For me, I've always struggled with King David. I wrote him off for years when I found out he was an adulterer. After my stepfather abandoned our family because of an affair, I wondered why anyone would take the words of David seriously. He became a member of the "bad men club" that existed within my head.

Not only did David commit adultery, but he covered it up with a murder. The woman he wanted to make his wife became his wife after David had her husband killed. Why on earth would I want to have the life and words of this adulterer and murderer speak into my life? The Bible felt out of touch and chauvinistic when it referred to David as a man after God's own heart (1 Samuel 13:14). Did it ignore his other actions to come to this conclusion? Surely King David wasn't all he was cracked up to be. How could someone who loved God *that* much mess up *that* badly? From my perspective, King David's life didn't even belong in the Bible. Wasn't there someone else more faithful to God whom God could have used?

David had highs and lows in his life, and a lot of his lows were because of his own doing. Yet David did a lot of admirable things too. As a young shepherd boy, David killed the giant Goliath of the Philistines, the enemy of Israel (1 Samuel 17). This was, of course, a noble act on behalf of Israel, and it showed me that maybe David did have a heart to serve God.

David was anointed king at a young age (1 Samuel 16) and crowned king over all of Israel (2 Samuel 15), but he didn't fulfill his role right away. God made a special covenant with David; as a result, Israel had peace (2 Samuel 7:8). David had to withstand persecution and unfortunate circumstances before he assumed his royal role.

David sinned in big things, like committing adultery and murder (2 Samuel 11), and in small things as well (2 Samuel 24; 1 Chronicles 21:1). Yet through it all, David repented. Maybe this is what made David stand out more than the rest. Perhaps he was a man after God's heart because he was aware of his own sin and knew his need for forgiveness. Maybe this is what God was trying to show me as I wrestled with David. That no matter how much I mess up—in big and small ways—God still loves me, and I can love and honor Him too.

God loved David, chose David, and had plans and purposes specific to David, in spite of the fact that David didn't live a perfect life. Despite David's shortcomings, God used him, and God can use me as well.

All of us sin, and God extends forgiveness to us time and time again. Even if we think we're relatively "good" people, we commit a colossal sin of pride and self-righteousness because no one is good but God alone (Mark 10:18). Not only does God know this about us and still love us, but He gives us opportunity after opportunity to return to Him. If we confess our sins to Him, God does not remember our sins or hold them against us (Isaiah 43:25; Jeremiah 31:34; Hebrews 8:12; 10:16–17), and He restores His relationship with us.

So how did David go from being an unnoticed shepherd boy to the rock-slinging slayer of an enemy of Israel and then to a king? David was the youngest in his family, so it was hardly his age that earned him a promotion. But not only did David's role change; his heart did as well. In order for our lives and names to change, we first must have a change of heart.

GOD CREATES NEWNESS INSIDE US

The book of Psalms is one of the most popular books in the Bible. The Psalms are read at weddings and funerals, and many people grow up with Psalm 23:1 (KJV) as their first Bible verse committed to memory: "The LORD is my shepherd; I shall not want."

David wrote Psalm 51 after his adulterous relationship with Bathsheba. I struggled with David as a Bible character when I looked at his life in isolated incidents. We tend to do this to people in our lives too. We disqualify people because of one sin or one hurtful act instead of looking at them as a whole person who desires to be loved despite their sin.

Yes, David messed up big-time. Yes, his sin is inexcusable. But if I long for God's forgiveness for myself, I must extend this same goodwill toward others. After openly confessing his sin, David offers an authentic prayer for mercy and forgiveness:

Have mercy on me, O God,
according to your unfailing love;
according to your great compassion
blot out my transgressions. ·
Wash away all my iniquity
and cleanse me from my sin.

PSALM 51:1–2

This prayer is about as honest as you can get before God. And you have to respect any person who can acknowledge their sin and ask God to forgive it. Not enough of us are aware of our own sin, let alone ready to ask forgiveness for it.

Psalm 51 is a beautiful prayer of confession and repentance. David is admitting his wrongdoing. He is not minimizing it, nor is he avoiding it. God is at work in the midst of David's repentance, and this is why David can ask for purity and still be considered a man after God's own heart instead of a murderer and adulterer. God was personal with David, and David shows us we can have a personal relationship with God.

Psalm 51:10 reads, "Create in me a pure heart, O God, and renew a steadfast spirit within me." This verse sticks out to me. An impure man who committed an impure act of adultery asks God to create purity inside him. How could that happen, as his life was anything but pure? Here is where I believe David gets the new name "Pure."

Some time ago, I prepared to teach at a purity conference before an audience of young women. The organizers asked me to give suggestions for modesty, along with Bible verses about how women of God should act and dress. I found Psalm 51:10 as I was preparing to teach—"Create in me a pure heart, O God, and renew a steadfast spirit within me"—and I researched what *pure* meant. When I found out, my entire outline changed. No longer was purity a checklist—a list of dos and don'ts and the "right" things to wear—but it became another miraculous work of God in our lives.

The Hebrew word for "create" in Psalm 51 is *bara*, which means "to create something from nothing." It is different from other forms of "create" in Scripture. *Bara* is a creating that only God can do, and it refers to His creating something out of nothing.

Bara appears in Scripture only two times. The first is in Genesis, when God creates the heavens and the earth literally out of nothing. Only God can *bara*-create. Only God can take nothing and make it into something. You and I can create, but we cannot make something from nothing. The only two times God *bara*-creates are when He makes the world out of nothing and when He creates purity and newness inside us (Psalm 51:10).

We cannot create purity or newness inside us apart from God. We can try to wear the right clothes, listen to the right music, and hang around the right people, but this will not make us pure or rename us. We can look pure on the outside by external identifiers, but we are truly new and pure only when God begins the purity process inside us. We need God to transform our hearts and minds to make us pure. And we need God to cleanse our sinful nature to give us a new name. Sheer willpower will not be enough to change us. Accountability groups will not be enough to transform us. Sunday school classes will not be enough to create a new name within us. Only God can *bara*-create inside us and give us a new name and a fresh start.

God creates this newness inside us in the same way He creates our new names. Memorizing Scripture will not manipulate God into giving us a new name more quickly. I wanted to be pure by checking off a list of wearing modest clothes and not fooling around with guys, but the emphasis of behavior modification is typically on ourselves, while in reality purity is God doing His work inside us. Only Christ's magnificent power and the Holy Spirit's sustaining presence can create and keep newness inside us.

When our faith becomes a list of things to do, we miss the grace of God, and we may miss hearing our new name. Our actions will not rename us. Only God can rename us.

NAMED OUT OF LOVE

As I continued to look into David's life, I paid special attention to the people who were affected by his sin. Bathsheba was the name of the woman with whom David committed adultery. Bathsheba became widowed when King David set up the slaying of her husband, Uriah, in battle (1 Samuel 11:15–17). David took Bathsheba as his wife, and the children born to them in Jerusalem were Shammua, Shobab, Nathan, and Solomon (1 Chronicles 3:5).

David and Bathsheba's second son was Solomon—a name given to him at his circumcision, the time when a Jewish family declared the name of their son. The name Solomon is derived from the Hebrew word for "peace." It's a meaningful name when we consider that God wants us to pray for the peace of Jerusalem (Psalm 122:6). Solomon's name bore a promise for an entire kingdom.

Not only was David a man after God's heart, but his son's name also testified to God's love. When we get a revelation of our new name, we will not be the only ones it benefits. Our spouses and children will notice a difference. Our coworkers and relatives will see a change inside us. Becoming our new name has far-reaching consequences.

Solomon was given another name by the prophet Nathan: "[Bathsheba] gave birth to a son, and they named him Solomon. The LORD loved him; and because the LORD loved him, he sent word through Nathan the prophet to name him Jedidiah" (2 Samuel 12:24–25).

While we're unclear about some of the meanings of ancient

names, I want you to see that it was out of the Lord's *love* that Solomon was renamed. God calls us out of love and names us out of His love, and so it was with Solomon (Jedidiah). This new name, Jedidiah, meant "loved by the LORD." This name contains the same root as the name David—"to love." Jedidiah's name was given as a message from God through the prophet Nathan and may well have indicated God's favor toward Solomon's reign over Israel. We're told in Nehemiah 13:26 that Solomon "was loved by his God," and our new names are meant to display this same love.

Can you remember when God spoke a new name over you out of His love for you? Are you forgiven, accepted, beloved, or strong? Wallowing in our sin or putting too much emphasis on our human nature can detract from the new life God has given us. Do you believe that you please your heavenly Father and that you are an heir of His, or do you wonder how He sees you and thinks about you? People of other religions wonder how their God sees them, but followers of Christ have been told we are named and saved out of love.

If our new name is attached to our sin, our shame, or the shifting sands of the culture, perhaps that's a label we're listening to instead. If your new name isn't given by the only One who has everlasting love for you, you may be living by a label that limits you.

ONE NAME FROM HEAVEN WILL HELP GET YOU THROUGH

The name Deborah means "bee." On the plaque in my best friend Deb's one-bedroom backhouse in California, the name is defined as "seeking one." Deb became my best friend when I moved to California, and I've known her in every season to be busy as a bee, seeking after God.

My friend Deborah took a job at a church in California, where she's in charge of building teams and community. She connects people to one another, manages the guest and usher teams, and is known as someone who's never met a stranger. She is friendly, upbeat, and fun!

Each year I've known Deb, she's gone away on a silent retreat with God and asked Him for a word or name for the year. I have known her to be called "Beloved," "Precious," and "Provided For." I have known her to receive words like *believe* and (be a) *light*.

This particular year her word was *gift*. When she is given a new name or word by God, she looks for ways that God will honor it throughout the year. There is nothing mystical about this practice; rather, it helps Deb remember God. I'm always challenged by how Deb's one word for the year encourages her when life gets hard. It helps her stay on track and reminds her that God is personal in knowing her.

The year Deb was given the word *gift*, she faced an unforeseen health condition. Deb is healthy and active. She cooks fresh meals and grows vegetables in her garden in the California sunshine. Doctor visit after doctor visit could not establish why Deb had extreme fatigue and unbearable pain in her stomach and lower abdomen. Deb was losing hope fast, and she was wondering where the gift was in that season.

Deb held on to her word, *gift*, and she began seeing God's gifts to her through the provision of people. A chiropractor who attended her church gave her free chiropractic care. A man in the church covered the cost of her medical bills. One family gave her homeopathic medicine and oils to help ease her pain. Several friends gifted her with travel to bring her joy when her body ached. Deb was seeing her word *gift* at work in her life, and she was reminded that every good and perfect gift comes from God above (James 1:17).

Deb's health declined for seven years. It was a severe battle, as every year she fought to keep her joy. It would have been easy for Deb to rename herself "Sick One"—but she heard many more encouraging words throughout the years. Each year, God's personal words sustained her and helped her fight for health with hope and not fear.

After seven long years, she wondered if she should still go on the personal retreats since her body was fatigued and her workload was full. Then she heard the word *whole*. Deb received complete healing when she was just about to give up. It would have been easy for Deb to quit, but knowing her new name year after year helped her remain focused. When she was tempted to rename herself "Sick," "Weary," and "Discouraged," Deb kept hanging on to the words God would give her. Are we willing to persevere and ask God to give us strength the whole year through? God has a personal name for us that will help prepare and sustain us when life gets tough.

Many of us keep looking for lists of things to do or ways to be obedient. We want God to speak to us and answer us. I've felt this way many times. I've prayed, "God, I am *serving* You, but why am I not *hearing* You?" But God is not a genie in a bottle, nor does He work on our timetable.

If God can make something out of nothing and create purity within our hearts, surely He can give us a beautiful and noble new name without us performing correctly. The dozens of name changes in Scripture were given to men and women who did not deserve this newness in God. God changed them *in spite of their sin*, not because of their goodness. Biblical name changes have everything to do with what God sees inside a person and the work that God does to change their heart. Our name change is not about what we can do for or offer to God.

Check out how many times in Scripture something happens for the sake of God's name. Our new names should put God and His transforming work on display, not us. If God made this beautiful earth—the rocks, trees, sand, oceans, mountains, hills, and plains—out of nothing, surely God can create a new name and a new family legacy inside us. Only God can give us a new name worth waiting for.

I had the opportunity to meet the beloved pastor Eugene Peterson at a conference in New York City. He was a humble man who poured into many pastors younger than himself. In his book *Run with the Horses*, Peterson writes about the prophet Jeremiah and how important a name is.

The book of Jeremiah begins with his personal name—"The words of Jeremiah son of Hilkiah" (Jeremiah 1:1)—and it's followed by eight other personal names. Did you ever notice how many names are in the Bible? Peterson writes that "our names are far more important than trends in the economy, far more important than crises in the cities, far more important than breakthroughs in space travel. For a name addresses the uniquely human creature."[8]

Peterson makes this point not because he discredits a person's occupation; rather, he sees deeper than an occupation and believes a personal name means something and reveals something. He goes on to say that knowing our name comes from a personal relationship with God.[9]

Having a personal relationship with God is the first step to knowing our true names and becoming ourselves. Our relationship with God gives our names substance; the identity He speaks over us gives our lives meaning and our future its direction. What is a name, after all, if not a sacred word spoken lovingly over a life? It is in our God-given name that our entire life finds its fullest potential.

David was called king by God long before he took this position. David was made pure before his actions could display it. Jeremiah's name had "the LORD" in it, the personal name for God, indicating that Jeremiah's parents wanted his life to count for God. But just as God had significant names for the saints of old, He has a new name and a new heart ready and waiting for you. Are you asking Him for it? Are you believing His new name is better for you than your actions deserve? Will you let God bring meaning, purpose, and purity to your name?

God names us, and as He chooses our name, He puts Himself on display, not our works. Our heart transformation and name-changing process are the very things that give God glory and introduce His saving grace to the world. He will be faithful to bring to completion this personal process inside you (Philippians 1:6). Ask Him to do it!

BEING RENAMED TO REFLECT YOUR PLACE IN GOD'S FAMILY

Rob and Karen Shive are a wonderful couple who have done full-time ministry for decades. Both licensed counselors, the Shives have helped numerous families. I met the Shive family at church when I was in high school and began mentoring their oldest daughter, Jessica.

The Shives had three beautiful biological children. And as strong as this family was, they felt someone was missing. After years of prayer and preparation, the Shive family began the adoption process and were paired with a beautiful girl in an orphanage in China.

The orphanage named their daughter Zhong Xiao Chun. She went by Chun, which means "spring." Naming is a meaningful process when an adoption takes place, and it looks different for each family. Some families keep a version of the child's birth name, and some change their name altogether. It's a tricky thing to honor the culture your child is from while also giving them a name that makes them feel they belong in your family. There is no right or wrong decision; it's simply something that takes discernment because naming is such a significant and meaningful process.

The Shives brought their daughter home and fell in love with her immediately. She was given the name Kelsey, meaning "ship's victory." The Shives gave her a new Chinese middle name, Xiao Mei. Xiao means "little," and Mei means "beautiful."

Kelsey was their beautiful little one, and their family felt complete.

Naming this child was one of the very first things done to acknowledge Kelsey's place in the family. Giving Kelsey a new name helped her fit in at school, and her last name tied her to her older siblings, whom she is very close to. When Kelsey took the last name of Shive, it was legal proof that she was a Shive family member.

The naming process sets children apart as belonging to their parents, and it should set us apart as those who belong to God. God has new names and identities for children who stay in orphanages, and new names and identities for children who are adopted into families. Our new name is meant to call out who we will become. Our new names are proof that we belong to God, and that He is personal to us.

Kelsey Shive lives up to her new name. She has victory in many areas of life as she follows Christ and serves her church. Kelsey leads her high school soccer team to victory with her natural God-given talent. She is no longer an orphan; she is a highly favored daughter! Kelsey didn't pick her parents; her parents picked her. So it is with our relationship with God. He chooses us, adopts us, and delights in making us His! Your new name will reflect who you are in God's family.

YOU BECOME A NEW CREATION

Since coming to the realization that I labeled King David by his sinful actions rather than as a new creation in God, I've discovered many ways in which his life now gives me hope. When I labeled David an adulterer, I couldn't see his heart of love toward God.

When I labeled David a murderer, I couldn't see his heart of faith and spirit of obedience to do the hard things God called him to. When we write people off based on the labels we assign them, we miss out on an opportunity to see the image of God in them. We miss out on seeing others as God sees them.

God does not look at our outside appearance; rather, He looks at our hearts (1 Samuel 16:7). If we belong to God and He has given us the name "Son" or "Daughter," we are no longer defined by our sin and shame.

When God saves us and renames us, he makes us a new creation. The apostle Paul talks about this in his letter to the church in Corinth: "Therefore, if anyone is in Christ, the new creation has come: The old has gone, the new is here!" (2 Corinthians 5:17).

After realizing God can rename people and give them a fresh start, I began rereading David's words, songs, and laments, and they taught me how to pray honestly before God. Where I had previously written David off as an adulterer, I now saw his rawness and vulnerability before God. David's prayers hold nothing back from God, and I realized that David had a more authentic relationship with God than I did. God would rather we put Him on display, even by vulnerably repenting of our sin, than make up a new name on our own.

Since only three things are eternal—God, the Word of God, and the human soul—we may as well practice seeing people as their new names and not as who they once were. Don't we want people to give us the same benefit of the doubt?

When I saw David as forgiven and created anew by God, I began relating to him instead of resenting him. I began to see him as a person rather than identifying him with his sin. When I looked at his name, I could let go of his sin that led me to judge him and define him—roles reserved for God alone. We can learn something from anyone who is moving toward God. We don't have to stay stuck in their (or our) wrongdoing for long.

David became one of the greatest kings in Israel, and knowing his new name—"Man after God's Heart"—allowed me to see him as such. David stepped into his God-given calling while facing adversity and even death threats from Saul—the man who was king of Israel at the time. As David ran for his life from Saul, I related to him, since I had to endure threats from my biological parents. It seemed that the biblical character I had avoided for years was being used by God to help me live out of my new name. Scripture was becoming personal to me, providing a road map for how to persevere. When I saw David's ability to serve and follow God, I stopped looking at David's wrongdoing and self-serving actions and listened to what God had to say about him instead.

Our former self goes away when the Spirit of Christ indwells us and God makes us into someone beautiful from the inside out. We begin to see ourselves in the stories of the Bible. Not only can we relate to people we've previously written off, but we can see how their names and stories all point to the name of Jesus Christ.

LIVING OUT OF YOUR NEW NAME

Around the same time I gave King David another chance, I was preparing to speak at a women's conference. Before I approached the platform to deliver a message, a woman preformed a skit with a powerful message about her husband who had cheated on her. When this woman found out the devastating news, she felt called by God to pray for her husband's repentance. After she had prayed for years, and with no restoration in sight, their daughters, also heartbroken because of his actions, also began praying. This family needed God to create purity inside a marriage that seemed broken beyond repair.

This family was in the audience to tell the end of the story. The husband realized what he had been doing was wrong, and years later he repented from his actions and desired to be restored to his family. Our churches are full of testimonies like this—imperfect people giving glory to a deeply personal God who creates a new heart, new spirit, and new name within them.

Following their testimony, I walked to the podium and taught about how God gives us a new name that supersedes the labels of our past mistakes. At the end of the sermon, I asked the audience to think of the new name that God may have for them. After my session ended, this family approached me at the front of the church. The husband said, "Today my name changed from 'Adulterer' to 'Faithful Husband.'"

Even though this husband and father had lived in repentance for years, he struggled to see himself as forgiven and new. He had a hard time forgiving himself for his years of unfaithfulness to his wife and the devastation it caused his family. Even sharing their testimony at church was a painful reminder of his sin and past labels. But on that day, something new happened. He knew his name was no longer "Unfaithful," "Absent," "Selfish," or "Failure." The name he heard for himself was "Faithful Husband," and his outlook changed.

This man received forgiveness when he repented of his sins, but he received hope and comfort from God after hearing his new name. I knew nobody was happier to hear his new name than his wife and daughters. Not only did this husband and dad need to hear his new name from God, but his family members who were wounded needed to have hope that this change was real and lasting.

REFUSING TO NAME OTHERS BY THEIR SIN

When people wrong us, it's easy to talk about their sin as if it were their name—and a bad name at that. For example, we say, "That person is a liar" or "He is prideful" or "She is selfish." Yet

defining a person by a single action strips them of their person-
hood. Can an entire human being—their history, fears, hopes, and
future—be captured fairly in a single label? I certainly hope my
identity doesn't hinge on one sinful action. So let's not name others
falsely by labeling them as their sinful actions; let's see them as a
whole person who has a name given to them by God.

God does not name us by our sin. What if instead we began
praying, by name, for the person who has wronged us? In doing so,
we shift our focus to God and His ability to create a new name in
even our enemies. What if we did this for those we disagree with
on Twitter? What if we got to know people's stories, fears, and
setbacks before assigning them to a philosophical or theological
camp we may not align with? Getting to know people's names and
stories is a way to honor the God who created them. Labeling and
gossiping about people is not the way of a Christian.

When we sin against others, what if we ask God to create a
newness inside us? What if we ask God for help to forgive ourselves? We cannot teach others their new name if we aren't willing
to believe that God has one for us too. What new thing is God
doing inside you? Ask others to speak into this question. What
new vision has God has given you? Pursue it. By all means, get
healing and forgiveness. Seek restoration or reconciliation with
others, but don't stay stuck in their sin or your sin when God
has a new name for you. If you were an adulterer, stop acting
like it and start acting like a faithful wife or husband. If you're
struggling with comparison and feeling "not enough," make the
conscious choice to log off social media for a while and practice
gratitude, knowing that God names you "Enough." We all need
second chances. We must choose to see what God is doing inside
us rather than focusing on what we've done.

I'm glad that King David didn't stay an adulterer forever. I'm
glad he asked God to *bara*-create something new in him, and that
his name and legacy changed. Generations hang in the balance of

your knowing and living out of your new name. David went on to have children, even within a relationship that was birthed out of sin. And Jesus, the only sinless human being, came into the world from the line of David:

> "When your days are over and you rest with your ancestors,
> I will raise up your offspring to succeed you, your own flesh
> and blood, and I will establish his kingdom. He is the one
> who will build a house for my Name, and I will establish the
> throne of his kingdom forever."
>
> 2 SAMUEL 7:12–13

If David could have a fresh start and positively affect generations, so can we. What if we start believing our new names and what God says about us in such a way that future generations will know about this newness that began in us?

I was discouraged, trapped, and feeling sidelined by God, and now I have confidence that God wants to use me. I was not liked by my biological family, but now I know I am liked (and loved) by God. I was beaten down and left out, and now I am determined to see others and build them up.

What about you?

Those past failures and losses that I used to identify with? They no longer describe or define me. It's not that I don't struggle with sin and wrong labels; it's that I no longer live by them and I refuse to take them on as my new name.

I used to experience anxiety whenever doing something new, and now I am brave. I was a people pleaser, and now I am able to communicate my feelings without fear. I used to keep a record of wrongs, and now I delight in the freedom that comes with forgiveness.

We have the privilege of pursuing God for our new name, which comes with a responsibility to believe what He says about us. He can give us the courage to live out of our new identity.

YOUR NEW NAME PUTS EMPHASIS ON THE NEW WORK

What is the emphasis of your current identity? Our name emphasis reveals who we are following and who we believe in. If your name is "Adulterer," your focus may still be on your sin. If your actions are full of anger and impatience, you may be forgetting God's ability to make all things right. When our emphasis is on our past circumstances, it's in the wrong place. And this doesn't just apply to those of us who fall short day in and day out. We need to check the emphasis of our name if it is always revolving around ourselves or our lists of rights and accomplishments.

All of us need a fresh reminder of the *bara* work of God—that He alone is the One who can create newness and goodness inside us. He makes us a new creation and gives us a new name. Do our names reflect where we came from or to whom we belong? Do our names reflect whom we used to serve, or do they point to the One we are currently following?

In our journey of discovering our new name, God will shift the emphasis off ourselves and help us see the new work He is doing in our lives.

> "See, I am doing a new thing!
> Now it springs up; do you not perceive it?
> I am making a way in the wilderness
> and streams in the wasteland."
> ISAIAH 43:19

God is not going to make a new way for us and then keep us captive in our old names and identities. We are a new creation in Him (2 Corinthians 5:17), and surely He will give us a new name when we ask Him to begin this work.

When we begin to see people as God sees them, we take on

a teachable posture. I began relating to King David when I lost a close friend (Psalms 41:9; 55). I found David's words helpful to ignite new hope inside me. Not everyone likes the new us. Not everyone can celebrate our new name. I have found that true friends stick with us in the new names. Some friends are there when we struggle, and others when we succeed, but the truest friends are those who know our labels but urge us to live in our new name. These are the friends I can go to when I'm tempted to believe old labels that lie and when I forget what my new name really means.

When we receive a new name in God, we become teachers and encouragers. We proclaim the new work that God has done inside us, and our testimony brings glory to God and hope to others. A lot hinges on our new name. A lot hangs in the balance of which identity we choose to live out of.

Living out of our testimony is different from naming ourselves out of the worst parts of our past. There will be challenges in the name-changing process, but there are struggles and setbacks in anything we seek that is worthwhile. Don't stop short of the new name God has for you. God wants to do a new work inside your heart. He can create a new name for you when nobody else sees new and good inside you. Your sole focus needs to be on Him at work in you, not on you making it happen yourself.

Eugene Peterson writes, "A personal name, not an assigned role, is our passbook into reality."[10] I wonder how you can seek God and ask Him for your personal name.

1. **WRITE DOWN:** Get away with God, like Deb did, and ask Him for inspiration. What is He doing inside you? Who are you becoming? Read through the names at the end of each chapter and write down the ones that resonate with you. How can you look ahead for what God has for you?

2. LISTEN: Maybe you've struggled to hear acceptance from your parents, but can you get alone with God and ask Him to speak a name over you? Skim through chapters 2 and 3 and see some of the names that are given to all believers. Do any of them stick out? Maybe you're being called to exchange your name of "Ugly" or "Unloved" for "Beloved" or "Accepted by God." Take on this new name. It is not arrogant; it is a testimony to a very personal relationship with a very personal God. He wants to speak good things over you. Listen to Him!

3. READ: Is there a person in the Bible you can relate to? What is it about their character change that resonates with your story? Read their story and see how God delights in making them new. Notice that God does not speak down to them but calls them to something better than what they were experiencing before.

4. ASK: Look at your current situation. Who can you ask to call out irrevocable gifts inside you? Who can affirm what God is doing inside you right now? Maybe you have a gift of empathy or compassion that is desperately needed in this world. With whom can you process a new name and identity? God often speaks through people!

5. IDENTIFY: Sometimes we have a hard time hearing our new name, because our old names are on autoplay inside our heads. What old name have you clung to? "Forsaken"? "Forgotten"? "Used"? "Unloved"? Ask the Holy Spirit to show you the wrong name you've been living out of and to replace it with something new.

6. REFLECT: What is God doing inside you right now? Is your new name right in front of you?

The Christian life fluctuates from desert seasons to mountain-top experiences, from obedience to disobedience. In 2 Samuel 1:11,

David led his nation in a lament that pleased God. Just ten chapters later, Scripture says that David displeased God (2 Samuel 11:27). So it is with all of us. We honor God and we disappoint God, but He does not call us by our sin. Recognition of our need, sin, and brokenness isn't meant to depress us; rather, it's meant to help us see that we are completely dependent on Him.

Have you given up on yourself or on the possibility of being a favored one of God because of your sin? Don't give up on yourself before your new name comes. When you're tempted to give up, realize that your emphasis may be on yourself rather than on God's power to transform you on the inside.

Many names throughout Israel's history included the name of God. Josiah's name means "The LORD heals." Joshua's name means "The LORD saves." Jehoiakim's name means "The LORD raises up." Your new name is personal to you, but it puts a very personal God on display. Who knows? Perhaps living out of your new name will be the very thing that introduces someone else to our very personal God.

Reflection: Is God personal to you? How has He transformed you? What part of your life do you need Him to create purity in?

Prayer of Blessing: You are a personal God! Thank You for choosing me! Please help me to surrender fully to You. I confess to You that for too long I've been trying to do things on my own. Please create purity and newness inside me. Give me a transformation of heart like David's, and allow me to sing to You again. In Jesus' name. Amen.

Verses to Believe: 1 Samuel 16:7; Matthew 23:25–26; Ephesians 2:10; also read through the book of Psalms to see how David prayed to God in a *personal* way.

Labels That Limit
Circle which of the old labels you have believed about yourself.

Adulterer	Murderer
Angry	Sick One
Beaten Down	Sidelined by God
Discouraged	Sinner
Forgotten	Trapped
Forsaken	Ugly
Impatient	Unloved
Jealous	Used
Keeper of Record of Wrongs	Vengeful
Left Out	Weary

Your New Name

Circle which of the new names you want to live out of.

Accepted	Man/Woman after God's
Adopted	Own Heart
Beloved	New Creation
Brave	Person of Peace
Confident	Pure
Delights in Freedom That	Strong
Comes with Forgiveness	Thankful
Enough	Used by God
Faithful Wife/Husband	Whole
Forgiven	

PART 3

Your New Names Benefit You and Others

CHAPTER 9

How to Live Out of Your New Names

He who was seated on the throne said, "Behold, I am
making all things new." Also he said, "Write this down,
for these words are trustworthy and true."
REVELATION 21:5 ESV

At the same conference where a man told me his name went from "Adulterer" to "Faithful Husband," a woman approached me and shared about an abortion she had during her teenage years. Since becoming a Christian decades later, she deeply regretted this decision. She carried guilt and shame in her heart every day. Even though she was now a mother of two children, she never forgave herself for ending her baby's life.

With tears in her eyes, this woman told me she took "Murderer" as her name. Can you imagine carrying this name around on a daily basis? While attending her children's choir concerts and volunteering for their school's PTA, she hoped nobody would find out her secret.

Our old names and identities are too heavy to hold on to forever. God wants to call us a new name and give us a new identity when we become His. God will not name us out of shame, as He sent His Son to the cross to pay for our sin and shame, and God will not name us based on our past if we have a new life in Him. It was clear that this woman was living out of her past and needed God to give her a new name.

I asked this woman if she had asked God to forgive her, and she said she had—many times in fact. It's at this point of confession and repentance that God gives us a new name. God would not continue to call this woman—His daughter—a murderer when Jesus went to the cross to pay for her sin. Now was the time for her to forgive herself and ask God to reveal how He really saw her. Many of us forget this important step in our walk with God. We want our past to be over and done with, but God wants to give us a new name to live out of as we move forward.

We don't just confess and repent and move on. Instead, we watch and listen for ways God makes us new. It is so like our loving and forgiving God to name us by who we will become, not by our sin. Our new names should change the way we live.

The woman and I prayed together, and after we finished, she held her head up and said that for the first time in her life she felt clean. She told me that since her abortion she had struggled with anger and a crushing guilt that made it difficult to even look in the mirror. She would respond with anger toward her spouse and hostility toward her children. But hearing this new name from God would make a world of difference.

Yes, the abortion had grieved the heart of God. And God has a name for her baby. But when this woman took on the new name "Christian," God had a new name and identity for her. God would never taunt her with her past, and her new name would give her the ability to see herself made new in God's eyes. Instead of seeing herself as "Murderer," she could begin calling herself "Forgiven" and "Clean." God will never tease us or make fun of us. He names us out of His love, not for our past.

This woman told me she struggled with anger in her parenting. Deep down, it was because she felt she didn't deserve to be a parent. She felt the name "Murderer" fit her better than "Mom," and subconsciously she had been parenting out of this name for years. Imagine how her new name, "Clean," would help her on a daily basis. Think of how empowering this new name would be. Over time, this newfound freedom would allow the anger to subside and her new names, "Forgiven" and "Clean," to take root.

Our new names will help us live better and freer than the lies we've settled into. This woman's new name, "Clean," put God on display, unlike her old name, which was a constant reminder of her sin. She looked at me with tears in her eyes and said she was leaving this conference a different person. She couldn't wait to go home and hug her children and tell her husband how she had been made new.

Knowing our new name helps us live in a different way than we did before. Believing differently about ourselves helps us treat others differently too.

YOUR NEW NAME AFFECTS GENERATIONS

Repentance and forgiveness come before our new names are given. But let us not forget that the next step is to share with people the good news that God can make them new too. You are no longer your past, and neither are they. It is a "both/and" walk with Christ. We repent and are forgiven *and* we are given a new name. We are not forgiven to stay stuck in our old names, old ways of thinking, and old patterns of behavior. It is because of Christ's death and resurrection that God can see the best of Christ inside us and not count the worst of our sins against us.

Bernadette is a brave military wife and mom who is raising her children to be brave for God in their schools and kind to others wherever they go. Moving can take a toll on military families, and as Bernadette relied on God for strength in the midst of another season of change, she felt the Lord tell her to be brave in this next season.

Bernadette looked up the meaning of her given name after a conversation with a friend, and to her surprise, she found her name means "brave as a bear." She got chills as she realized that the Lord wanted her to see the link between her given name and the way He wanted her to live it out. Sometimes our new name is right in front of us!

I've noticed a trend among spouses—from military parents to business leaders and surgeons—to rename themselves "Single Parent" when their spouse is gone or working long hours. Many times one parent does bear the brunt of the child-rearing while the other works outside the home to support the family. Not for a second do I want to minimize the accomplishment it is to parent with only one person present, but I do wonder if we do damage to ourselves and our spouses when we take on a name that really isn't ours. Have you ever thought about how your children feel when they hear you speak of your new name?

Not only does the name "Single Parent" not bring honor to the spouse who is away, but this name does not highlight how brave you are to do your job and how brave actual single parents are! What's more, calling yourself something you are not may bring heaps of pain to the single moms and dads who are sacrificing greatly to be present and to provide for their children. Our children (and the next generation) are listening!

Bernadette focused on her name, "Brave," instead of naming herself incorrectly. Holding on to her name in a season of change helped her remember that God was with her to help her. She didn't need to wrongly name herself "Single Mom" to give herself more credit or draw attention to her circumstances. Living out of her name, "Brave," allowed her to shine the light on Christ and how their family would survive another difficult transfer.

Living out of her true name also served as an example to Bernadette's children, who took on a posture of prayer when their father was gone. They no longer joked about him being gone or acted out sarcastically or negatively. Instead, they became grateful for their mother's and father's sacrifices to keep the family provided for.

When we live bravely, we give others courage to live the same way. When we live loved, we point to the One who gives unconditional, unending love. There is no doubt about it—people watch the way we live and pay attention to the names we live out of. Is the name we take a testimony of bravery, courage, and faithfulness for future generations to see? Or do they see us as those who complain, fail to show gratitude, and live bitterly as a prisoner of circumstances and pain? Sometimes living out of our new name means looking at what is right in front of us and not believing a label that tells us we're behind in life or have somehow missed the mark. Bernadette's new name was wrapped up in what she had been called for years. Is God's name right in front of you too?

BEARING UP UNDER CULTURAL PRESSURE

When I attended a secular university, I faced name-calling for being a Christian. Certain groups labeled me "anti-women" because I didn't support abortion. I was called a "prude" when I stood up to my professor who was advocating we live with our boyfriend or girlfriend before getting married. Living in this world can be confusing, and knowing our new name can help us discern the times we live in (Luke 12:56) and distinguish good from evil (Hebrews 5:14).

The Old Testament book of Daniel tells the remarkable story of a young boy, most likely a teenager, who was taken captive by an emperor named Nebuchadnezzar. A professor at Oxford University, John Lennox, writes, "What makes the story of their faith remarkable is that they [Daniel and his friends Hananiah, Mishael, and Azariah] did not simply continue the private devotion to God that they had developed in their homeland; they maintained a high-profile public witness in a pluralistic society that became increasingly antagonistic to their faith."[11] How did young Daniel survive and honor God when a foreign culture turned against his name?

Lennox's book, *Against the Flow*, details the social engineering practiced by the Babylonian society, and one of the first attacks was changing a person's name. Names were very important in the Hebrew culture, signifying something the child would possess, live up to, or become. The book of Ecclesiastes says that "a good name is better than fine perfume" (7:1).

Daniel's name means "God is my Judge," and his three friends taken captive with him also had Hebrew names with special meanings. Hananiah's name means "The LORD shows grace." I love to see the truth that "God shows grace" displayed throughout the Old Testament. Mishael's name means "Who is what God is?" This was, of course, a rhetorical question, as God is God, the Lord over all, and there is none like Him. Azariah's name means "The LORD helps"—a statement of God's character that is seen throughout Scripture.

All four of these men had Hebrew names with meanings that glorified their God. Their names spoke of God's goodness and character. Their names were intentional and were part of their destiny.

One of the first things that happened to these young men after their capture was that their names were changed. Though their names testified to the character and nature of God, the empire that held them captive wanted them to serve another god, and so their names were immediately changed.

Pastor Chris Hodges addresses these name changes in his book *The Daniel Dilemma*: "By comparing the original and Babylonian names of these four Hebrew young men, we get a clear picture of our Enemy's strategy, the same one he uses on us today: he labels us with a new name so he can lie to us about a false identity."[12] God has a new name for us, and so does the enemy. And when someone attacks our name, they are most certainly trying to influence our identity.

Daniel, Hananiah, Mishael, and Azariah were given Babylonian names that stood in direct contrast to their Hebrew names. Many scholars believe this was more than just the Babylonians' attempt to rename them; it was an attempt to wipe the name of the God of Israel from their hearts, minds, and legacies.

We learn how to live out of our true identity from the lives of Daniel and his friends. Daniel's name was changed to Belteshazzar, which means "Bel, protect his life!" Bel was a foreign god, not Daniel's God. All throughout the Old Testament, the God of the Hebrew Scriptures is seen as a God of refuge and strength to His people. He is an ever-present help in our time of need (Psalm 46:1). Daniel was going to need to rely on God's strength and protection during his life, and here the enemy, through Daniel's captors' renaming of him, tried to divert his attention to another god. This god, Bel, could offer no help or protection for Daniel. The goal of this renaming was to cause Daniel to forget his God.

Hananiah was given the name Shadrach, which means "command of Aku [the moon-god]." Mishael's name was changed to Meshach, which means "Who is what Aku is?" And Azariah's name was changed to Abednego, which means "servant of Nabu [Nebo]," another Babylonian god (see Isaiah 46:1). All four of these name changes were attempts to blot out the name of the God of Abraham, Isaac, and Jacob and divert attention to other gods—a goal still being pursued in our culture today. Forsaking our God-given names has so many implications, including causing us to forget the one true God.

The same threats will come against you. What is the enemy trying to steal from you? Are you willing to believe that God is good and has good names for us, and will you hold on to that truth when the culture says otherwise?

When I first learned of these name changes, I was surprised. I had heard the story of Shadrach, Meshach, and Abednego in Sunday school but had never connected these men as Hananiah, Mishael, and Azariah—their God-given Hebrew names. I knew these men had survived after being thrown into a fiery furnace, but I didn't know the struggle they went through to maintain their integrity when they were incorrectly named by the culture around them. I was unfamiliar with the courage of Daniel and his friends as they lived in this hostile society.

Knowing and maintaining our new name is an important part of how God's story continues for the next generation. When we know our new name, it will help us withstand the culture that tries to rename us "Fools." We live out of our new name when we listen to God and endure in a culture that tries to blot out the name of the God we serve.

YOUR NEW NAME WILL HELP OTHERS

On a work trip to New York City, I crossed paths with a woman my age named Emily, who is a Jewish believer in Jesus. She has taught me a lot about the Jewish roots of my Christian faith.

As we were getting to know one another, Emily commented that she loved my name, Esther. She said that the name Esther has significant meaning in her life. Emily's father's name is Richard, but his Hebrew name is Joel, meaning "Yahweh is God." Emily and I found it interesting to see the overlap of names in our families that grew up on opposite sides of the world.

Although Emily has a Jewish father, she wasn't given a Hebrew name at birth. Her dad rejected his religious upbringing, and her mother isn't Jewish. This caused Emily to feel left out when she was with her Jewish friends. Her parents divorced soon after she was born, and as she grew up, she rejected her Jewish heritage. Emily spent most of her life trying to have as much fun as she could, partying and abusing alcohol and drugs. In Emily's words, she lacked any true peace, purpose, or identity.

In the Jewish tradition, words have significant meaning. Genesis teaches that God created the world through His word. Judaism teaches that every letter in the Hebrew language is sacred, and therefore the name of something (or someone) reflects its distinct characteristics and the purpose for which it is created. It's customary for Jewish parents to give their children Hebrew names at birth along with their Western names.

The Hebrew name is believed to embody the unique character traits and God-given gifts of a person. It is used in the synagogue and at special occasions, such as marriages or bat/bar mitzvahs. Jewish people are encouraged to use their Hebrew names on a regular basis. When Emily was asked what her Hebrew name was, she would have no answer. She felt it caused her to lose credibility in Jewish circles, where she desperately wanted to belong.

It's easy to reject important parts of our heritage if we don't have our identity rooted in an unchanging God. In the midst of Emily's university years, even though she had Holocaust-surviving grandparents, she became very anti-Israel. She wrote a paper in her final year that condemned Israel, but during her birthright visit to the country, she had a transforming encounter with the God of Israel, where everything changed, including her name.

As Emily started getting to know the God of the Bible, her

identity was being formed. She began asking God for a Hebrew name. She knew how important names were in her culture, and she wanted God to give her a Hebrew name she could live up to.

As she read the Bible, the book of Esther jumped off the pages. Emily went to Israel to celebrate Purim, a holiday that began in Queen Esther's time as she was used by God to save the Jewish people. Emily found herself an outfit fit for a queen as she walked the streets of Jerusalem, celebrating how God has kept His eye on the Jewish people, and still does to this day. Although Emily's earthly father did not give her a Hebrew name, her heavenly Father gave her the name Hadassah, Esther's Hebrew name, and told her to celebrate it, exhorting her to live boldly and courageously as a Jewish believer in Jesus.

Emily now works for one of the oldest and largest Messianic Jewish ministries in the world. She is a light to the Jewish people and reminds them that when they accept Jesus as Lord, they don't need to give up their Jewish heritage or their Hebrew name.

Emily is secure in her new name. God has shown her His heart for the nation of Israel and His love for the people, both Jew and Arab. When her Jewish friends ask her what her Hebrew name is, she no longer sheepishly answers that she doesn't have one. Just as Queen Esther was spared from physical death, Emily went from spiritual death to spiritual life in God, with a new name to show for it. Emily's newfound identity helped preserve her Jewish heritage and the beautiful story that God continues to write for the Jewish people.

You may not have a Hebrew name, but what work has God done inside you? Has God given you courage like Esther's to live for Him? Has your faith been put through the fire, like Daniel's was? Did you feel the culture was trying to rename you, like it did Daniel and his friends, but now you have courage to stand unashamed of your faith? God wants us to hear our new names and truly live.

Maybe God changed you from being a spin artist to being a truth-teller. Or perhaps your name was "Enslaved to Sin," and now it's "Freedom." Maybe you were known as a cynic, and now God has transformed you to have the gifts of encouragement and faith. Is there a Bible character you relate to and aspire to be like, as Emily did with Esther?

We can open the pages of Scripture and see a great Hall of Faith of people we can strive to be like. The people we read about weren't perfect, but God isn't expecting perfection out of us. If you have a new identity in Christ, you have a new spirit inside you and a testimony of the new things God has done!

YOU NEW NAME HELPS YOU REMEMBER GOD

To this day, the Jewish people retell the exodus story during Passover, remembering they were once slaves whom God brought out of Egypt. In the same way, we will need to tell God-stories over and over again to tell of His faithfulness and of how He has renamed us. How can we remember the ways God has rescued us, fighting to remember our identities and new names in God? What if the Jewish people forgot to tell the exodus story over and over? What if they failed to remember the reason for Purim? Thankfully, we have these true stories to remind us of a faithful God.

I need my husband to call me his bride and remind me of his love for me on a regular basis. It sounds funny, but what if we said, "I love you," on our wedding day and never again after that? All of us need reassurance in our relationships and new names. When my husband reiterates his love, it helps me make it through those days when I feel undesirable, unwanted, and unloved.

While you don't need a spouse to remind you of your identity, you will need *somebody* to remind you. Maybe you have an aunt or grandmother who has always believed in you. Maybe you have a pastor or boss who sees things in you that you can't yet see for yourself. We're all fragile when it comes to believing we are who God says we are. Daniel had good friends, and he needed them to stand with him. Queen Esther had a relative who reminded her of her identity and helped her be unashamed of her heritage. We all need meaningful relationships to remind us of who God says we are, and it's okay if we have to ask God for a reminder too!

WHO'S YOUR DADDY?

Even though I faced ridicule in some of my university classes, I was also Luther Elliss's adopted daughter. I walked on campus in the confidence that Luther and Rebecca knew me and loved me. I knew they would support me if I faced ridicule and teasing, and I knew I'd come home to being loved by their growing number of children, my siblings. Knowing who I belonged to helped me endure name-calling and gave me courage to live out of my new name.

When people mess with our names, they are messing with the core of who we are. Our names are sacred identifiers. So when others want to attack our names, they'll have to take it up with the God who named us in the first place, and He will never back down.

Whose son or daughter are you? If you belong to God, you belong to Him and receive protection and provision when people come against you. God speaks meaning and purpose over your name and destiny.

To grow in our Christian walk, we need to maintain a personal relationship with God, with His Word, and with His people—the church. But some of us can get so busy with Christian activities that we forget to maintain a relationship with God Himself! May we not get so distracted by serving God that we forget to ask Him to speak to us personally. Every one of us needs to hear love and affirmation from our Father God! Are we setting ourselves up to hear our new name from God, and are we living it out?

POST-TRANSFORMATION PRAISE

A lot is at stake if we forget our God-given names. Forgetting our new names can cause us to forget our identities. Forgetting our new names can cause us to forget where we came from or where we're heading. Even worse, forgetting our new names can cause us to forget the name of God. When Daniel's and his friend's lives were spared, Daniel said, "Praise be to the *name* of God for ever and ever; wisdom and power are his" (Daniel 2:20, emphasis mine).

God's name is lifted up when we withstand the attacks that come against us. God's name is exalted when we believe we are who He says we are. God's name gets attention when our outward names demonstrate the inner work He has done in our hearts. We don't have to be missionaries or government legislators for our names to make an impact on the next generation. Our new name and God's work inside us are meant to be an eternal work and an eternal testimony to a God who names us out of His love.

Daniel praised the name of God, and as we live out of our new names, we give glory to God's name too. Our new names benefit us, yes, but they also give hope to others and focus attention on the name of God. How has He made you new? Your new name is worth remembering—no matter what.

HOW TO REALLY IMPACT THE CULTURE

The world around us will not understand us. Most of them will not be able to recognize the new creation and celebrate it. Few friends will be throwing parties for you after you have a revelation of your identity in Christ. When my friend Matt gave up a lifestyle of drugs to follow Christ, he was no longer invited to parties and was cast out of his friend group for being "weird," "different," and "too spiritual." We ought to be prepared for opposition from a world that will label us as "fools" (1 Corinthians 4:10).

When we hear our name from God, however, we can live courageously when labels that limit us come our way. Instead of taking these labels to heart, we can realize that the attack against us is actually against the One who names us and lives inside us.

My friends Jay and Katherine Wolf are great examples of people who live out of their new names. Katherine suffered a sudden brain stem stroke shortly after college. Jay stayed by his bride's side as doctors fought for her life. Katherine was on life support for forty days, and by God's grace, she survived. Jay was tempted to take on the names "Hopeless" and "Despairing," yet he fought with hope and prayer for his young bride. Katherine courageously battled for her life and for joy, persevering through two intense years of brain rehab. The labels Katherine was tempted to believe were "disabled," "hopeless," and "will never be the same."

This couple had a long road to recovery. They're proof that our new names don't always come easily or quickly. Katherine had to learn to talk and walk again. And while she returned home with a body that didn't work like it once did, she had a renewed hope, an undying spirit, and a confidence that God was not through writing her story.

This couple has persevered to live out of their new name. They were given the name "Hope" and started a beautiful ministry called Hope Heals. Jay and Katherine have two strong sons and travel the country to share their story of suffering with hope. Physical limitations have not stopped them; instead, they are determined to live with hope and inspire others to do the same. Hope Heals now holds summer camps for families of disability. They have challenged countless others not to focus on the label "disabled" but to find their ability and blessing from God. Knowing their new name—"Hope"—helped Jay and Katherine live abundantly again, and this confidence has helped them give hope to countless others.

Can someone look at your limitation and call it freeing? Can someone look at your disability and see you as joyful and strong? If someone has heard of your recent diagnosis, would they call you confident in God? When the worst has been thrown at us, do we believe that God is with us, still has good names for us—even in dry seasons—and wants to give us the name "Overcomer"?

God wants us to live out of our new names as post office workers, business professionals, nonprofit volunteers, and schoolteachers in the same way He wants pastors and missionaries to live. Even strong, capable, do-it-yourself kind of men need to receive a fatherly blessing and name change. A new name is available to all of us who are in Christ, and God desires that we live out of our new name in a way that has a positive effect in the culture around us.

Remember whose you are, and pray for courage like Daniel's to take a stand for God's name in a culture that wants to rename you. Remind yourself of God. Holding fast to what is good (1 Thessalonians 5:21) includes maintaining our God-given identity and living out of our new name.

For Further Reflection

Reflection: How does the next generation hear you talk about your name? How can you take a stand for the name of God in the culture He has placed you in? How can your new name give courage to others? With whom can you share your new name?

Prayer of Intercession: Heavenly Father, thank You for refreshing me. Help me to refresh others. Help me to realize that my new name does not end with me. You are writing a much bigger story than the one that begins and ends with me. Help me to align myself with what You are doing in the earth. Bring into my path others who need Your love. Show me how to represent You and how to lead them to Your name—the name that is above every name. Amen.

Verses to Believe: Proverbs 11:25; Ephesians 5:21; Philippians 2:3–4, 13; 2 Thessalonians 1:11

Labels That Limit
Circle which of the old labels you have believed about yourself.

Adulterer	Murderer
Complainer	Prisoner
Cynic	Prude
Despairing	Single Mom/Dad
Disabled	Spin Artist
Enslaved to Sin	Too Spirited
Fool	Ungrateful
Guilty	Weird/Different

Your New Name

Circle which of the new names you want to live out of.

Brave	Faithful Husband/Wife
Christian	Forgiven
Clean	Free
Courageous	Loved by God
Daughter/Son	Peaceable
Encourager	Truth-Teller

CHAPTER 10

We Overcome

No, in all these things we are more than conquerors through him who loved us.

ROMANS 8:37

As I continued to work out my new last name, Esther Allen, my husband and I began discussing children. There can be an immense amount of pressure in the faith community for newly married couples to have children. It shows how we are never satisfied as a human race. When you're dating, people want to know when you're getting engaged. When you're engaged, people want to know when you're getting married. Within seconds of the completion of your wedding ceremony, people want to know when you'll start having children. Since Joel and I were in our thirties when we got married, we knew the questions about children would come fast and furious from friends and family.

Intellectually I believed children were a blessing (Psalm 127:3). Spiritually I knew that God called men and women to be fruitful and to bear children (Genesis 1:28). But emotionally I didn't feel ready. My fear that I'd become a mom like the mom I'd had overwhelmed me. Sometimes we can overidentify with our wounds in a way that paralyzes us, but God wants us to move past seasons of brokenness and look for the new thing He is doing in our lives.

I took a long, hard look at my fear of having children. Unfortunately, we don't get a free pass to ignore Bible verses we are uncomfortable with. Children are a blessing, and God gave me a husband. It was time to stop identifying as Esther Fleece, the girl from a broken family with a broken past. It was time to create a new family cycle and a legacy for generations to come.

A few months into our marriage, I heard my husband praying out loud for me while drinking his morning coffee in the front room. My husband, the best man I know, was talking to God about his desire to have children. He was praying for my body to be able to bear children, and asking God to bless our family by increasing us in number. It's hard to be unmoved when you hear somebody praying for you—even more so when it's your husband, the person you love more than anyone in the world.

Rather than being annoyed with him for praying for something I didn't feel ready for, my spirit was awakened to the reality that I was the one who could help him see his prayers answered. I was *the* woman who could fulfill his desire to have children. I wanted to see my husband's prayers answered, and I wanted to bless him with children, even if I was afraid of becoming a mom.

I had anxiety about the name "Mom." I knew it was a big responsibility and a role that would require my attention for the rest of my life. I've been known for starting things—clubs in school, companies in my twenties. But parenting is a job that requires you to start and end well. Maybe if my husband believed I could be a good mom, he would also be the support I needed to excel in this calling.

We need others to speak over us what they see in us, even before we can believe it for ourselves. About the time Joel and I started to pray together about whether to begin having children, God used little children to affirm that I would be a good mom. Both my Elliss siblings and my Elam siblings sent me random texts telling me they loved me and believed I'd make a good mom. It's amazing to see prayers answered through little (and teenage) children.

While there was no guarantee I'd be a good mom, and certainly no guarantee I could have biological children, I began asking God if the name "Mom" was a name He had for me. I started praying, "God, is one of my names 'Mom'? Is this a name You have for me?" I was scared to pray these prayers. I felt I knew God's answer before I even asked Him, but I needed to take my fear and anxiety to Him and let Him bear the weight of my fear.

While I didn't receive an audible answer, I was given peace about trusting God. While I didn't know what our story of childbearing would be, I wanted God to lead our family in this and every area.

I kept this prayer silent in my heart, much like Jesus' mother Mary pondered things in her heart (Luke 2:19). It felt like a deep and risky prayer. I was reluctant for people to hear this prayer, and I didn't want to fail. What if we couldn't have children? What if I miscarried? What if I wasn't a good mom? Would this new name and calling mess up my career?

I brought my husband into my fears and prayers, and he processed these things with me. Our new name is not only about us; it affects other people too. If you feel stuck in an old label or unsure that a new name is for you, take time to process it with another person. Just as my husband needed me in order to become a dad, I needed him in order to become a mom. We are created to need each other in this name-changing process.

A few weeks after hearing my husband pray for me and seeing God change my heart, we celebrated my thirty-fifth birthday. I was in a busy season of teaching and speaking, and we took a weekend trip with our friends Brett and Tiffany to celebrate my birthday over dinner. After I'd had to go back to the room several times throughout the day because I didn't feel well, our friends looked at us during dinner and said, "You guys, you know you're pregnant, right?"

Of course we didn't know we were pregnant! The thought hadn't even crossed our minds. I'd seen prayers go unanswered for years, even decades, and I was anticipating this prayer might take years and tears and heartaches too. While it's good to be patient in our years of waiting, it's also refreshing to see our prayers answered quickly. It's part of God's process to build our faith back up again.

Tiffany took me to the nearest grocery store, where I bought my first pregnancy test. I was shaking in line at the checkout counter and wanted to make sure the attendant saw my wedding ring. I had never been so nervous as a grown woman before. We hurried back to the hotel room, and the test came back positive within seconds. I found my husband, and we cried. We couldn't believe we were getting the new names "Mom" and "Dad."

DON'T OVERIDENTIFY WITH YOUR WOUNDS

Our stories are important. They are part of our testimony about what God has done for us, including the old from which we've come and the new to which we're called. But there's a second part to our stories. How are we overcoming? How are we being made new? What is God doing in us, not just yesterday or last week or ten years ago, but today? Do our stories show God's ongoing faithfulness?

When we stay in our old names, identifying with our old stories, we make the name-changing process about us. Yet this process is not about us; it's about God revealing His name to the world and revealing Himself through our stories and the people we are becoming.

Scripture reminds us that God is doing a new thing (Isaiah 43:19), and some of us need new stories of how God changes us. Some of the most refreshing people to be around are those who have recent stories of God's faithfulness and answered prayers. I'm moved every time I see a gray-haired believer raising their hands in worship at church. It gives me hope that if they can testify to God's ongoing goodness, I don't have to lose my fervor either.

And because this process is not about us, we don't need to go through it alone. I imagine Sarai was left alone in her thoughts when she decided to ask her husband to sleep with her slave Hagar so Sarai could become a mother. Being left alone in our thoughts is a dangerous place to be. We begin conspiring about how to manipulate people or circumstances to make our new name or calling come about instead of leaving it in God's hands.

Yet we are never left to our own resources. If we're walking with God in the newness of the Christian life, God will constantly be teaching us and transforming us. He strengthens and equips us every day to live into our new identity. He knows it's a big change from our old story. He has compassion for us in this major transition and leads us step by step into a new story that's even better than we could have imagined.

Maybe your old identity was "unwanted" and "abandoned." Will you trust God to lead you into your new identity as "chosen" and "cared for"? Maybe your old story was feeling like a misfit. Will you trust God to lead you into a new story of belonging? Or maybe your old name was "Guilty." Will you choose to believe God's new name for you of "Forgiven"?

Leaning into your new name is a lifelong journey that requires God's ever-present help. These names and God's work inside you do not go away but rather continue to build stories of God's faithfulness. Our testimonies are ongoing, but our labels are not meant to be carried forever. Let us gather in His name (Matthew 18:20) and process the change going on inside us. Our identity is the truest thing about us, and we are meant to be known and cele-brated and to bring glory to God.

Nine months of preparing for our baby gave me adequate time to begin to believe the realness of one of my new names—"Mom." I went from doubting I could become a good mom to believing God would give me everything I needed to be the best mother for my son. I chose to throw off the old lie that I wasn't good enough, smart enough, or equipped enough and trust that God would be present with me in my parenting. I watched fears like "having a child could hold me back in my career" give way to praising and thanking God every day that this son could be the focus of my affection.

Pregnancy was a great example that we need time to marinate in our new God-given names and identities. Yes, God can change our identity in a millisecond, but it will take us time to learn how to live in newness. We bring our fears, anxieties, old names, and labels to God, and He shows us His truth that grounds us.

Nothing on earth could have prepared me for this experience. Of course I read books, listened to podcasts, and did my best to prepare, yet nothing could have armed me with what I needed for living out of this new name. It was more beautiful than I antici-pated and rawer and more vulnerable than I was prepared for. There were so many spiritual parallels to painful seasons of wait-ing, deferred hope, and suffering that feels like it will never end.

Childbirth was good for my faith. I saw that pain, however long, does eventually come to an end. I saw that suffering produces good fruit—physically, emotionally, and spiritually. I saw that it was good to not be alone in my pain. I needed helpers—and I had my strong husband, a doula, nurses, and a doctor there to help me. I saw that I was expected to call out for help in my pain instead of trying to prove that I was strong.

My faith took on new meaning. I couldn't help but think about how God gave His Son for me. I didn't want to let our boy out of my sight. He wouldn't sleep apart from me for weeks, so I sat in a recliner, sleep deprived, just to make sure he felt safe and secure. How much more does God not slumber or sleep as He watches over us?

And while I am keenly aware of wonderful women who will not have this experience, I want to tell you that when God births a new name in you, it will be a beautiful process. It may take time. It may not look like you thought it would. There may be pain along the way. You will need helpers and encouragers. But the birth of your new name is intensely beautiful, and this process is meant for every single one of us. God does not withhold good from us (Psalm 84:11), and He is birthing something new in you.

There will be a temptation to overidentify with our new names too. We can make good names and good titles into our identity and end up worshiping the gift of a new name rather than the One who gave us this gift. I could be tempted to make my new name "Wife" or "Mom" ultimate or more of a priority than my name "Child of God." But our names are about God and are meant to tell of what He has done inside us, not to draw attention to ourselves.

When we submit to God's leadership in our lives, there is no name of His gifting that is impossible to take on. He wants newness, freedom, love, kindness, gentleness, and more to radiate out of whatever name we take on. Some of us will undergo seasons of sorrow and suffering, but we are promised that these will not be our names forever. If we make God the foundation of our identity, the only One who is unchanging (Hebrews 13:8), we will hold steady through the highs and lows that come our way.

DO YOU HAVE A NEW SONG?

Lisa Harper is a great example of God birthing new seasons and names within us. When she was in her fifties and single, she adopted a beautiful daughter. Lisa knows the love of God and shares His love with others as a Bible teacher and speaker. She has a kind and generous heart and felt God lead her to pursue the adoption of a little girl from Haiti. Some might label Lisa "unmarried" or "too old" to have her first child, but God was birthing a beautiful new name in Lisa and also in her soon-to-be little daughter.

God is not limited to the plans we have for our lives or to our natural circumstances. Just this week, I received a call from a friend who wrestled with infertility for ten years. She just found out she's pregnant with her third biological child. Against all odds, God has new names and seasons ahead for us. We won't always escape suffering and get a happy ending or the child we desperately want, but God will put a new song in our hearts when we endure.

Lisa went on to adopt her "precious pumpkin" from Haiti, and her daughter has filled her home with joy. Her daughter, Missy, was malnourished when she brought her home, and now she is provided for. She was HIV-positive in Haiti, and now her scans show a full healing. This dynamic duo radiates the beauty of a God whom we can trust to birth new seasons in our lives.

When God does a new work inside us, our lives will sing again. Psalm 40:3 says God "put a new song in my mouth, a hymn of praise to our God." When God lifts us out of the "slimy pit" and out of the "mud and mire" (Psalm 40:2), He gives us the ability to sing again. This new song and season come after a season of despair. If you are in a despairing season, take hope that a new season is around the corner.

The psalm goes on to say, "Many will see and fear the LORD and put their trust in him" (40:3). And so our new song isn't about us or our circumstances; our new song is about living out of our true identity as a child of God, causing others to see the Lord and put their trust in Him. It's why we refuse to make good things, like children, ultimate things. And it's why we have confidence that despair is not our final song.

A new song is a powerful outworking of living out of our new identities that soon prompts others to lean into their own. Our son's name is Asa, which in Hebrew means "healer." God put a new song in our hearts through the birth of our son, and we knew we would never be the same. God has used my son to heal my heart of my mother wounds and fears. God has used my son to help me forgive my biological father, and God has used him to redeem the name "Mom" in my life. What new song does God want you to sing? How has He renamed you or birthed something in you that has changed you for the better? The next generation needs to hear your new song to the Lord.

The transformation God does inside us is personal and starts with us, just like childbirth, but it does not end with us. God changes us from the inside out, and because this transformation is for His glory and not our own, it has ripple effects in the lives of others.

A SONG OF HEALING

I had no idea how much being a mom would require of me. I was unprepared for the sleepless nights, sheer exhaustion, and constant feedings that never gave my body a break. But there was beauty in the mundane too. I thought about God's constant provision for and protection of me. I thought of God's love for me in calling me His daughter and not leaving me as a stranger or slave.

One morning as I was changing my son's diaper, I began singing the Apostles' Creed to him. While I didn't know a melody for this old Christian creed, I made one up.

> I believe in God, the Father Almighty,
>   creator of heaven and earth.
> I believe in Jesus Christ, his only Son, our Lord,
>   who was conceived by the Holy Spirit . . .

My son looked at me, and my heart filled with joy to be his mom. In that moment, I remembered that my father had taught me this old Christian creed when I was a little girl. Night after night, he would make me recite it with him as I lay in bed ready to go to sleep. I remembered one particular instance when he sang this creed and said it was the foundation of our faith and of the utmost importance that I memorize it.

I guess I did memorize it, and here I was singing it to our son.

I had completely forgotten this memory with my dad and began to sob. My dad *did* care for me at one point in time. My dad *did* love me, even though he didn't know how to show me his love. And in this moment of forgiveness, I was renaming my dad.

He was absent, but I could remember when he would put me to bed. He was unstable, but I could remember his presence. He was violent, but I could remember days when he didn't act that way.

When my father's mental illness took over, the devastation stuck with me more than the beauty that proceeded it. We all tend to remember the bad over the good. But in this moment, I started to see my father as loving instead of as a monster. After decades of asking God to help me forgive him, I was forgiving him—right then and there—as I changed my son's diaper. I picked up my son, just two months old, and held him in the rocking chair and sobbed.

Who was my father through God's eyes? What did God name him? He was a husband, a father, and a son. At one time, he was God's son, until he forgot God and made Him in his own image. My father was a deeply distressed man. He was mentally unstable but not unlovable. God cares deeply for those with mental illness, even those who do not seek help for it. And God cared for my father, even when his actions caused me harm.

I began to thank God for the new names I could see in my dad. I could see that he tried to raise me in the faith and had introduced me to God and the church. I could give thanks for these things and for the few good memories I had of him showing me love.

As the weight of unforgiveness began to lift, I thanked God for giving my son a good father. My husband is everything I wanted my father to be for me. He is present with Asa. He is encouraging, steady, and strong. My husband is intentional with our son and sings to him and holds him close. My eyes were being lifted away from the old brokenness, and I was able to thank God for the new wholeness I was experiencing through my new family.

Families are holy vessels of God. They are meant to flourish and reflect the relational God we serve. But since the fall of Adam and Eve, every single family is a broken family. Even the most God-loving and God-fearing homes come with dysfunctions and unhealthy habits and need God to set them on a healthy path. While many of us have hurts as part of our family stories, we're not meant to overidentify with these wounds; rather, we are to build a brighter future for the generations beyond us. We are meant to overcome and to create cycles of health, not perpetuate cycles of brokenness. We are meant to be agents of a new way forward, with God's help.

HOW TO BECOME MORE THAN A CONQUEROR

Paul's letter to the Romans is one of the most glorious and complex books in the Bible. Romans 8 is about life with the Spirit of God. Paul says our present sufferings are not worth comparing with the glory that will be revealed in us (verse 18). It says that even creation waits in expectation for the children of God to be revealed (verse 19). If creation is excited to see God revealed through you, imagine God's delight in bringing about this process inside you.

So much of Romans 8 is applicable to us as we face pain and are called to persevere as sons and daughters of God (verses 22–25).

The good news is that the Spirit helps us in our weaknesses and even with what to pray for (verse 26). No part of this Christian life—the renaming process, the changing of our identities, the transformation of our hearts, the living it out—none of it is on us. We are to depend on the Spirit of God to change us and make us new, and we need others around us to live it out.

But what does it mean to be "*more than* conquerors"? "No, in all these things we are more than conquerors through him who loved us" (verse 37). Isn't being a conqueror enough? Isn't it enough to say we have overcome? Isn't it enough just to know our new name? Why does Paul say we are *more than* conquerors?

When we are given a new name or move past the dreadful names we have clung to, we overcome. Some of us have overcome abuse, abandonment, divorce, infidelity, poverty, and more. Others of us are overcoming difficult seasons, circumstances, and pasts.

Being *more than* conquerors means that whatever the enemy did to take you out—whatever was meant to destroy you—did not in fact destroy you and is now being used for the glory of God.

You are a conqueror when you overcome sin; you are *more than a conqueror* when you use this testimony for the glory of God. You are a conqueror when you move forward in your new name. You are *more than a conqueror* when you forgive those who have incorrectly named you. You are *more than a conqueror* when you live out of your new name and sing a new song of how God has transformed you.

The New Living Translation puts it like this: "No, despite all these things, overwhelming victory is ours through Christ." We are not just conquerors; we are *more than conquerors* when we live out of our new names. The victory is overwhelming.

Do you hear it—God's new name for you? I hope you'll try it on right now. In His eyes, because of His Son, you are *more than a conqueror.* May this be the beginning of a lifetime of belief.

GOD USES YOUR UNIQUE CIRCUMSTANCES

My former orphan heart was choosing family. God was giving me a new song and helping me forgive my father and heal from his loss. I was choosing family and forgiveness. I was trusting God and leaning into the new names He was giving me. My suffering and my past did not have to separate me from the love of God.

My past identity as an unloved daughter was meant to take me out. But because of God's great work, He turned this identity around. He not only healed me but turned my past identity into a powerful new identity meant for His glory.

A survivor of sex trafficking needs a new name, not just a rescue. An inmate needs a new name, not just parole. Each of us needs to be restored after a season of loss.

And what about you? What was thrown against you and meant to take you out? Where did you see God's rescue? Can you tell others so they can find hope as God changes them too?

Our pain does not define us, nor is it meant to be a ball and chain that follows us until the day we die. God is doing a new thing. His new thing and your new name are meant to change the world.

Overcoming is about looking ahead and realizing that what was meant to destroy us was destined to fail. We are alive and have received grace for today, so God must be at work. If we are His children, He wants us to be more than conquerors, no matter what is thrown our way. Overcoming is about drawing a line in the sand and declaring that our past can no longer define us and rule over us. It is about acknowledging that God is doing a new thing and giving Him an opportunity to work through us. God gives us a new name, a new song, and a new hope as He makes us a new creation. This hope is meant to propel us forward, not lead us to dwell on the past.

YOU ARE STRONGER
THAN YOU THINK

One of my best friends was adopted when she was nine months old. She was given the name Tamy, which means "palm tree." There was no spiritual significance to this name, and she was born in Colorado, a place without any palm trees. And while her mother wanted to give her the best life possible, my friend experienced horrific sexual abuse at the hands of the father who adopted her.

It's a miracle to hear of any child overcoming sexual abuse. This abuse is horrific because it reaches inside us, where our identity, significance, and new names are formed. Adding to the horror of this sexual abuse was the fact that Tamy experienced it from her father. A father's love should be safe, affirming, and protective. How devastating to live in an unsafe home like this!

By God's grace, Tamy grew up to be a beautiful, kind, functioning adult. She and her husband committed their lives to God and began raising children of their own. Tamy soared in her love for God and began leading Bible studies as a new believer. With her husband's help, she courageously revisited painful memories, fighting to overcome and forgive, not just forget.

As Tamy grieved the pains of her past, she found comfort in an Old Testament Scripture. Isaiah 61 gave her courage to see how God could provide for her after a time of despair.

> He has sent me to bind up the brokenhearted,
>   to proclaim freedom for the captives . . .
> to comfort all who mourn,
>   and provide for those who grieve in Zion—
> to bestow on them a crown of beauty
>   instead of ashes,
> the oil of joy
>   instead of mourning,

and a garment of praise
    instead of a spirit of despair.
They will be called oaks of righteousness,
    a planting of the LORD
    for the display of his splendor.

                    ISAIAH 61:1–3

God was providing for Tamy after her time of loss. He was restoring to her what was taken from her. God was giving Tamy a faith of her own and a beautiful family to create new memories with. Tamy was a victim of horrific abuse, but she did not live like a victim. She leads mission trips to Jordan and the Middle East, offering hope to women who have experienced abuse. She leads a prayer ministry in which she bears the burdens of women who have faced similar abuses. Tamy walked with me in my own healing process and waited patiently with me as God led me from mourning to praise.

Tamy told me her new name is "Oak of Righteousness"—from the Isaiah 61 passage. She is no longer a palm tree swaying in the wind. She is firmly planted. She is strong. She is not easily shaken. God provided for Tamy in her grief and gave her a crown of beauty instead of ashes, joy instead of mourning. To this day, I laugh harder with Tamy than I do with anyone else on earth. Tamy is an overcomer, and her new name gives evidence of a divine Healer. Tamy gives thanks and praise to God instead of wallowing in despair and living out of her past abuse. She is an example of strength, and by living out of her new name, she gave me confidence to discover mine.

GOD NAMES THE NEW IN YOU

There is no formula for how our new names will come to pass. As I study the significance of names throughout the Bible, I find deeply moving testimonies and meaningful stories that reflect God's heart for His children, but no prescription for how it happens.

Our new names are given to us despite the many times we fall short. Our new names are given despite what has been done to us. God will see the *new* in us and call it out! He will call us to things beyond our wildest dreams and expectations. Our new name is for our good and is a testimony to the new thing God is doing inside us. Our new name will be good; we don't need to fear it. Our new name will be a blessing; it will not embarrass us. While our new name will show that we are more than conquerors, it is meant to put God's name on display.

And after God gives us our new name, we can begin to see the people around us—even those who have hurt us—with new eyes. Christ knew He was God. And because He knew His name, position, and authority, He was able to forgive, even as He experienced the most horrible abuse humanly possible. At the cross, Jesus said, "Father, forgive them, for they do not know what they are doing" (Luke 23:34).

How could Jesus see His offenders this way? How did He not collapse under these intense pressures? How could Jesus think of others in the midst of His last hours on earth? Jesus could look with eyes of forgiveness because He knew His name, and He knew His Father. As Jesus hung on the cross, He asked God to forgive the people putting Him to death. Instead of focusing on their wrong or calling them names they rightly deserved, He renamed their sin by pleading for their forgiveness.

What has this life thrown at you? Maybe it's the pain of rejection, the sting of betrayal, the death of a dream, the pang of loneliness.

Life has many ways of wounding us. But our God is the God of overcoming. We overcome not by ignoring our pain or pretending it never happened, but by asking God for the name He has for us instead of naming ourselves by the pain inflicted on us. You are more than the abuse you experienced, and it's not meant to be your new name. You are more than the betrayal you faced, and it's not meant to define you. You are more than the isolation you find yourself in. God wants to name you for the new thing He is doing inside you, not give you a name that reminds you of what has been done to you.

Your new name is better than you could imagine, because it is being written by a God who loves you more than you could ever imagine! Do you believe it?

For Further Reflection

Reflection: What has the enemy thrown at you that you want to use for the glory of God? Where have you almost quit, and why? Can you point out what can cause you to give up prematurely? Whom do you need to forgive?

DECLARATION: Write out your testimony in two hundred words or less. This is good practice for helping you become comfortable sharing your story with others.

Prayer of Thanksgiving: Thank You for being an overcoming God! Help me to take heart because You have overcome the world. I believe it is Your desire for me to rise above my circumstances. Help me to cast my anxiety on You because You care for me. Give me power to overcome. Thank You that my overcoming is not based on a change in my circumstances, but on Your blood. Help me to overcome evil with good and to share the testimony of what You have done inside me. Thank You for giving me the victory, now and forevermore! In Jesus' name. Amen.

Verses to Believe: Psalm 27:1; Isaiah 41:13; Romans 5:3–5; 1 Corinthians 15:57; James 1:20; 1 John 4:4

Labels That Limit
Circle which of the old labels you have believed about yourself.

Abandoned

Absent

Abused

Betrayed

Deeply Distressed

Despairing

Divorced

Guilty

Impoverished

Inmate

Isolated

Malnourished

Mentally Ill

Misfit

Monster

Mourning

Orphan

Scarred

Survivor of Sex Trafficking

Too Old

Unfaithful

Unloved

Unmarried

Unstable

Unwanted

Victim

Violent

Your New Name

Circle which of the new names you want to live out of.

Belong

Cared For

Chosen

Comforted

Crown of Beauty

Firmly Planted

Forgiven

Free

Garment of Praise

Gentle

God's Son/Daughter/Child

Image Bearer

Joyful

Kind

Leader

Loved

More Than a Conqueror

Mother

New

Not Easily Shaken

Oak of Righteousness

Overcomer

Radiant

Strong

CHAPTER 11

We Know His Name

"The one who is victorious I will make a pillar in the temple of my God. Never again will they leave it. I will write on them the name of my God and the name of the city of my God, the new Jerusalem, which is coming down out of heaven from my God; and I will also write on them my new name."

REVELATION 3:12

As soon as we found out I was pregnant, I began preparing for our baby—taking prenatal vitamins, praying over the baby in my womb, and absorbing information from books and podcasts. From *Baby Wise* to *What to Expect When You're Expecting*, no matter how much I prepared or educated myself, it all seemed to go out the window when I held our son in my arms for the first time.

Holding this little one in my arms changed me. It revealed my insecurities, insufficiencies, and fears. Becoming a parent was so much harder and more time-consuming than I ever imagined. There was always something new to learn and to absorb. Parenting is a beautiful, humbling, exhausting, ever-learning journey!

We were told early on to watch a flat spot on the back of our son's head. Some people say this could have happened as early as the womb or in the birth canal, and others point to the "back is best" sleeping philosophy. Whatever the cause, I took a season away from my work to do therapy with our son to loosen his neck muscles so he'd have a better range of motion to help his head form properly. And while we saw dramatic improvements, his head shape didn't fully correct on its own. No matter how much I read or prayed and even as I gave it all I had, our son still needed extra attention.

At our son's six-month checkup, the doctor wrote a prescription for us to see a cranial specialist. I made the appointment for the following week and was plagued with worry in the waiting. Was I the cause of this? Should I have caught this earlier?

The cranial specialist took photos of our son's head, and we waited anxiously for the results. Labels like "neglect" and "not a good mom" entered my mind. Even though I had never left our son's side, I felt like I needed to prove myself when I heard these labels lie. When we are not confident in our new names, we feel we need to explain ourselves to others.

Our son was diagnosed with plagiocephaly, which is a flat spot on a part of the head, and in that moment, no one needed to call me any names. I took on all the negative names and labels for myself. "Neglectful." "Bad Parent." "Failure." "Missed it." "Didn't pay attention to it." "My fault." "I could have done better; I should have done better."

I held our son on my lap and tried to listen to the analysis, but the labels that limit were so noisy that I couldn't retain a word the specialist was saying. The thing I did not want to become more than anything in the world was a bad mom. I wanted to break this generational cycle. The name "Bad Mom" was echoing in my mind, teasing and taunting me, and I wasn't able to get it to stop.

While I'm grateful for the technology available to help our son, I hated that we needed it. For the rest of the appointment,

I heard the name "Failure" when the doctor talked about our son's flat spot. I heard "Failure" when they showed us the 3D images. I heard "Failure" when they talked about the problems this flat spot could bring about, like a tendency to get increased ear infections. The physical therapist prescribed a medical helmet, and I left the appointment listening to labels and feeling utterly defeated.

SHIFTING YOUR ATTENTION

I know many of you have faced or will face much harder diagnoses than this, and so I don't want our attention to be on what our family faced. I want us to reflect on how these pesky labels confront us at every turn. No matter how prepared or prayed up we are, the enemy is like a roaring lion seeking to devour us (1 Peter 5:8) with labels that lie. The labels we fight don't always come from our past; sometimes they prevent us from becoming who God wants us to become.

Have you ever heard the name "Failure"? Maybe it has nothing to do with your children, but maybe you and your best friend had a falling-out. Maybe you didn't meet a major deadline at work or didn't pass an important test. "Failure" is one of the most common names the enemy will shout at us in opposition to God's desire that we walk forward in victory.

Was I a failure, or is my child loved, known, and provided for? Did I fail, or was this circumstance outside of my control?

In this moment, I needed to take my focus off myself and the lies I was quick to believe. I needed to shift attention elsewhere. I had to choose to believe what God had previously named me rather than the incorrect name, "Failure," that was vying for my attention. But how could I do this, practically speaking, when my world had been turned upside down and all signs pointed to my label and not my new name?

KNOWING GOD'S NAMES

Many of us forget that carrying God's name gives us spiritual benefits as His children. Knowing God's names is key to our overcoming as we shift our attention from our labels to the One who is greater. If someone is sent in the name of another, they carry with them the reputation and authority of that person. Think of an assistant who runs errands for their boss or a CEO who sends an e-mail on behalf of the company.

God's names carry authority, and we are to go in His name. God's names tell us who God is, and through them, we discover we have power to overcome labels that lie.

We are to revere the glorious and awesome name of God (Deuteronomy 28:58). But while some of us revere the name of God, we forget that the name of the Lord is a strong tower to which we can run and find safety (Proverbs 18:10).

When we look at the names of God and the power and truth they hold, we find strength and help in our time of need. When we know God's names, we can rely on Him more readily (Isaiah 50:10).

The devil loses power when he hears the name of Jesus (Luke 10:17), so we can pray in Jesus' name for His help to hear what is true about us. I pray this regularly: "God, please speak louder to me than the voice of the enemy. Rebuke the enemy's lies in Jesus' name." When we put our focus on God's name and our new name in Him, we will always have the victory.

When we live out of labels, our instinct is to turn to them in times of trouble. We look inward, and that's when our downward spiral begins. In ancient times, the psalmist wrote, "Some boast in chariots and some in horses, but we will boast in the name of the LORD, our God" (Psalm 20:7 NASB). Notice that the people of God boasted in the *name* of God. They found strength and refuge in the *name* of God, and when they won the victory, they praised His *name*. Before I knew the importance of a name, I skipped over the name of God, missing its power in both the Old and New Testaments. But this "name that is above every name" has always been there. While we may no longer boast in chariots and horses, we do boast in our careers, our health, our knowledge, and our earthly blessings. God would much prefer that we know His name.

THE NAME ABOVE ALL NAMES

God revealed his divine nature to Moses, a former orphan, and we reap the benefits of knowing one of God's names, "I AM": "God said to Moses, 'I AM WHO I AM'" (Exodus 3:14).

The name "I AM" encompasses everything. God is everything you need Him to be and more than you can imagine. God is perfect, unchanging, and unending. We could spend a lifetime searching out all that this name means and still not scratch the surface. There will always be more of God to know!

And look at how the names of God help us know our name! Knowing God's names helps us remove the labels that limit us and see our place as His dearly loved children.

If God is a provider (Philippians 4:19), then we are provided for. If God is our shepherd (Psalm 23:1), then we have a leader and a tender guide. If God is a protector (Psalm 91), then we are safe. When life gets distracting, shifting our attention to God's names will help us.

To boast in God's name means to have confidence in His name. The confidence we have in ourselves, in those around us, and in our circumstances will constantly be changing. But when we look to the names of God, we can be confident that He is everything we need.

Christian author Jen Wilkin wrote a book titled *None Like Him*, which takes the reader through ten ways God is different from us.[13] Wilkin writes about how our God is infinite, incomprehensible, self-existent, self-sufficient, eternal, immutable, omnipresent, omniscient, omnipotent, and sovereign. This was an important book for me to read when it was easier to believe the labels that were lying to me. It's good to realize who we are and who we are not. Our limitations are not weaknesses that leave us unworthy to be loved; they are entry points for God to do His work.

God is an ever-present help in time of need (Psalm 46:1), and when we know His names, we get a better glimpse of who we are and how we are provided for. God told Moses that His name, "I AM," lasts forever: "This is my name forever, the name you shall call me from generation to generation" (Exodus 3:15). How much more should we be focusing on His eternal name than on our temporal circumstances!

God is enough for you, forever. God is everything you need, forever. There is enough of God to help you in your time of need, and there is enough of God for your neighbor and lost coworker. God is not just present with you when things are going well; He is the "I AM" and all you need when everything is falling apart. Whatever circumstances you're facing and whatever season you're in, God's names will cover you and be your provision forever.

Search through the Bible to see God's name and the things He does for His holy name. Many times when I'm struggling, I will go to the Bible and focus on God's names. He is "Sovereign LORD" (Jeremiah 32:17) and a "great God" (Psalm 95:3). He restores us (Psalm 80:19), and He has strength and power in His hands (1 Chronicles 29:12).

God wants to be known as an everlasting Father to us (Isaiah 9:6), not one who leaves us to fend for ourselves. God wants us to know that His loving-kindness lasts forever (Psalms 118; 136). God wants us to have confidence that He is faithful, even when we are faithless (2 Timothy 2:13). Do you take the time to know His names and benefits (Psalm 103:2)?

God's names are important to Him. The beginning of the

Lord's Prayer acknowledges the holiness of the *name* of Jesus' Father: Hallowed be thy *name* (Matthew 6:9 KJV, emphasis mine). God does a lot for His name's sake. He guides us for His name's sake (Psalm 23:3). He forgives us for His name's sake (Psalm 25:11). He leads us for the sake of His name (Psalm 31:3). He does not want us to take His name in vain (Exodus 20:7).

Being aware of God in each situation we face helps us live for His name and not our circumstances. God matures us when we get to know His names and shift our attention from our labels and circumstances. We can invite the name of God into every part of our day, both the good and the bad, and trust that His name will carry us to victory.

I had time to reflect on our son's diagnosis before making some judgments. Was I a failure, or was he provided for? Was I a bad mom, or did I love him more than I ever thought was humanly possible? Did I cause this, or was God using this to teach me how to name myself correctly? Focusing on God's name brought me great peace, and when the day came for me to take my son in to get fitted for his medical helmet, I walked in with confidence, knowing that I was the best mom for him.

DISPLAYING HIS NAME

Our new names do not begin with us. Our stories begin with the One who is the divine name giver, God, who knit us together in our mothers' wombs. Our names—our stories—don't end with us either.

The lawsuit I faced pertaining to my biological father continued for two years. It brought strain to my marriage and stress to every day. We shelled out thousands of dollars to fight something that was outside of our control to begin with. I took comfort in the fact that Jesus faced wrong accusations and was misunderstood by family members, but I still experienced an enormous amount of grief, since I was at odds with family members I'd previously been close to.

During these years I struggled with labels like "forgotten" and "alone." Sometimes life is so busy and we have so many things to take care of that we forget to take a daily time-out to focus on God's names. When we focus on God's names, we gain clarity about who we are. And when we know who we are, we can fight for freedom and forgiveness. When we know our new names, we can even rename our offenders and those who have done the worst to us.

Knowing God's name is one thing; displaying God's name is another. A lot of us say we know the name of God, yet our actions don't necessarily show that we follow the name of God. Some of us focus on displaying the name of God and yet forget to grow in our knowledge of the names of God. Both are important, and both are lifelong journeys we are invited into.

This lawsuit became the catalyst that God used to help me forgive my earthly father completely. Instead of living out of the name "Abandoned," I began focusing on my new name, "Adopted." Instead of focusing on what I lost, I chose to give thanks for what I did have. What is thrown against us can actually be used to help us learn the names of God. This is how our trust in Him and intimacy with Him grow. We felt deep relief when we received word from our lawyer in Florida that we won the case, but a greater victory was learning to trust that I was being defended by God.

Because God had forgiven me of much, I was able to forgive my biological father. Forgiveness isn't for only the super spiritual; it frees every single one of us. When I focused on God's name and how He had forgiven me, I was able to see how God used this lawsuit to cause me to pray about my feelings toward my father every day for two years. I needed God's strength and help, and I needed to pour out my lament to God and ask Him for the courage to fully forgive. Knowing that God was my Father and focusing on the fact that He would be with me forever helped me extend forgiveness when the crushing weight of grief took over.

Because God accepted me, I did not need to wait for acceptance from an earthly father. I didn't even need a verdict in my favor to be evidence of God's favor in my life. Jesus experienced the full favor of God and died a gruesome death on a cross. Just because we don't receive the answer we're looking for or a promise we've been waiting for doesn't mean God's unending love toward us has changed. Sometimes our lack is meant to draw our attention to one of His names. Sometimes our unmet desires are the catalysts we need to take our labels to Him and hear how His grace is sufficient to meet us at every point of need.

Because God forgave me when I was at my worst, I could forgive the worst done to me. Because God is love, I can live loved, even when I don't feel seen, liked, or appreciated.

Psalm 20:1 reads, "May the LORD answer you in the day of trouble! May the *name* of the God of Jacob set you securely on high!" (NASB, emphasis mine). We are set securely on high, above every circumstance, when we focus on the names of God.

When we live confidently out of our new names, we are free to see the good in others, even those who have significantly wounded us, and cut them some slack. This is when the Christian life becomes paradigm-shifting and hard to live out in our own strength. But a renewed mind is exactly what a new identity produces. God changes us, and we cannot help but shift the way we think, speak, and see.

Living in a constant state of judging is a sure sign we are more fixated on labeling others than knowing our true new name. Living out of our new names takes time and constant attention. Focusing our attention on labeling others is an unhealthy way to distract ourselves from our own issues and needs. This is not the way of God's kingdom. God's way is to remove labels from people, and we are to be facilitators of that.

What would happen if we spent less time labeling others and more time focusing on the names of God? We may see our friends who have made unhealthy decisions as lost and in need of a Savior. We may begin asking God to pursue them rather than pointing our fingers in judgment. We may begin seeing the parents of wayward sons and daughters as hopeful and prayerful instead of sizing up their parenting skills. We may grow in empathy for people who are in dry seasons with the Lord instead of giving them a checklist of spiritual disciplines they should be practicing.

Focusing on God's names will turn us into the world's greatest encouragers. Living out of our new names will make us the most refreshing people in the world to be around. We will become less self-absorbed and leave a false sense of guilt behind us. Believing our new names will hel us be less concerned about mislabeling others, and we may even gain some unlikely new friends!

RENAMING YOUR OFFENDERS

Following the unexpected lawsuit, we received a small allotment of money as an inheritance. It was enough to cover our legal costs, and with a little left over, Joel and I prayed about how to spend or invest it. My initial desire was to go on a shopping spree to make up for all the birthdays and celebrations my father had missed. But I realized this would be a temporary high and fail to leave me fulfilled. What was one thing I could do to change my father's name and legacy?

We decided to put the remaining money into an account for our children's future education. This probably wouldn't be a lot of money to kids whose parents save up for their education, but this was a lot of money to me. Instead of being named "Broke" or "Unable to Pay Child Support," my father would be remembered for his provision to his grandchildren.

My father's name and legacy were being redeemed—not because I'm great at forgiving, but because God showed me a path to knowing my true name and living for His name. When we know who we are and whose we are, we can extend kindness and forgiveness to others, renaming them in the process. Which of your offenders need a new name?

Think of the story of Joseph, who was sold into slavery by his brothers. After years of not seeing them, Joseph could still identify them as brothers—though they could more appropriately have been labeled human traffickers. Yet after Joseph lamented what they had done, he could name them brothers, even when they didn't deserve it. Years down the road, Joseph could see how God used this tragedy instead of letting it destroy him.

God is using your tragedies and unexpected circumstances too. After Joseph was sold into slavery by his brothers, he worked for Potiphar, who was Pharaoh's guard. The Lord helped Joseph became successful in the house of the most influential man in all of Egypt (Genesis 39). It would have been easy for Joseph to live out of the name "Forsaken" or "Unwanted," but he focused instead on serving and knowing God. Living for God's name will one day prove all the labels wrong.

Not only could Joseph forgive his offenders, but he could rename them. A sure sign of our healing is when we can rename our offenders—the ones who slandered us, who unjustly fired us, who abandoned our friendship so quickly. If we focus on God, we can see that He uses even dreadful circumstances to teach us about His name.

Renaming the ones who have hurt us, sought to destroy us, or disparaged our reputation gives God the name "Justice." God no longer wants our offenders to name us. Instead, He wants to give us a new name, and the courage to rename *them*.

I started looking at the Bible to find other people who lived beyond their labels. Moses was orphaned, yet he led God's children out of bondage into freedom. Esther was orphaned, yet she grew

up to have courage. Hagar was abused, yet she is the one who testified to "the God who sees us." The people I studied in the Bible
were beaten, bruised, abandoned, neglected, subjected to slavery,
overlooked, and more, but they didn't stay that way. Each of them,
at one point or another, stopped looking at their dreadful labels
and instead embraced and lived into their new names.

We will all be hurt by people, and Jesus shows us how to be
unoffended and unafraid. Many times the wounds we receive will
come from people who are wounded themselves. Joseph was sold by
his brothers because of their jealousy and envy. Pilate found no guilt
in Jesus, yet he still sentenced Him to death. The wounds of others
can heap devastation and destruction on us. Sometimes the weight
can feel crushing. And while it hurts deeply, I want you to fix your
eyes on the only One who can give you an everlasting new name.

We will be in a spiritually healthy place when we can acknowledge the wounds of people who have harmed us and yet rename
them "Forgiven" rather than focusing our attention on their
wretched actions that caused us pain. We don't need to run and
tell them they're forgiven, by the way. This was some of the best
advice I ever received. Forgiveness is a process between you and
God, not you and them. Only by fixing our eyes on the name of
God, the One who will never hurt us or let us down, can we move
past harmful experiences.

When I focused on my absent father, I forgot his mental illness that was destroying his mind, which was deeply devastating.
When I focused on my mother's abandonment of me, I questioned
whether I would ever be accepted and loved. But when I could see
my parents as people who had experienced hurt themselves, I could
begin to forgive them. I could stop saying, "I hate them," and begin
to say, "I think they tried."

When I was labeling my parents "absent" or "abusive," I was
focusing on what was done to me rather than on what God
did for me. We do this all the time when we've been wronged.

But shifting our attention to God's names—"Compassionate," "Loving," "Caregiver," "Present"—is so much more freeing to us.

This doesn't mean we carelessly forget every offense or excuse every offender, granting them permission to reenter our lives. There are loads of books and resources dedicated to helping us find safe people and avoid toxic relationships, but I promise you that renaming your offenders will shift your focus from their offense and your wrong label to who God says you really are.

What if we begin to see our offenders as lost and in desperate need of God? What if we begin to see the people who have hurt us as hurting themselves and in desperate need of a new name from God? Seeing our offenders and violators this way doesn't give them a free pass for what they've done. I still don't have a restored relationship with my biological family members. And yet our new name empowers us to live in newness and extend mercy as God's children (Matthew 5:7). Can you give a new name to the person who has wronged you?

FOR HIS NAME'S SAKE

God wants us to tell future generations about His name and what He has done inside us. God does not want our old names and painful circumstances to be the end of our stories. The pain is part of our testimony, but the pain will not be our new name!

Our lives are meant to point people to an everlasting, unchanging, unconditionally loving God. The verse I picked out for my father's tombstone was Malachi 4:6—"He will turn the hearts of the parents to their children, and the hearts of the children to their parents"—and I was seeing this verse come true.

Even though my children would never meet my biological father, they could be provided for by him. I removed the name "One Who Never Paid Child Support" from my father and renamed him "One Who Provided for My Son." I exchanged his former label "absent" and replaced it with "present with the Lord." Because even after all of the pain and torment he caused me, I do believe my father was saved. I wasn't minimizing or ignoring the past; I began to watch for the ways God was going to redeem it. The redeemed of the Lord tell the story of their new name (Psalm 107:2); they don't put the emphasis on the sin.

God's names not only teach us who God is; they also inform who *we* are.

LIVING FOR HIS NAME

None of my early preparation for parenting equipped me to overcome anxiety. And as a Christian, I can sometimes wrongly label something "preparation" when it really should be called "worry." Worry doesn't go into a savings account so we can store it up and use it on a rainy day. Worrying takes away our joy and peace and clouds our ability to hear our new name.

Much of my preparing to become a godly wife, mother, and Bible teacher was actually bathed in worry and an inability to be confident in my new name. Would I be enough? Would I be a good teacher? Would I be a good mom? Worry can disguise itself as godly preparation. And while it's good to prepare, our ultimate victory has to rest with God (Proverbs 21:31).

Knowing our name is important for how we live, and knowing God's name is important for how we get the victory. Knowing God's names empowers us to live a Christian life. If we do things in God's name, for God's name, and by God's name, we get the victory and overcome.

The story doesn't end with us, and hearing our new name is only the beginning of living a life that brings glory to the One who has renamed us. Our names testify to a story that is bigger than all of us, and this is a beautiful thing.

We are to go and baptize in God's *name* (Matthew 28:19). We are to pray for and believe in healing that occurs in God's name (Acts 3:6, 16; 4:10; James 5:14). Everything we say and do is to be done in God's *name* (Colossians 3:17).

Knowing our name helps us know this God we serve. And knowing God's name helps us live like Him. When we take up His name as His children, we bear His authority (1 John 5:14–15), receive His inheritance (Ephesians 1:11), and watch Him make all things new (Isaiah 45:19; Revelation 21:5).

We will be like the psalmist who walks through the darkest valley, but we're never called to *stay* there. Rather, we keep walking. We look to where God leads us. He always leads us to victory. His path is one of life and restoration, forgiveness and freedom. So don't give up before your new name comes! Don't give up before the victory!

We are not just to *get through* hard seasons; we are to use them to discover our new name. There is a good chance that smack-dab in the middle of a hard season, a challenge, or a loss, God will speak (or sing) a new name over you. And if God speaks truth to us in these seasons (lawsuits, diagnoses, disappointments, discouragements, and more), we can take our eyes off our circumstance and start finding a new name that belongs to Him—one we didn't know before.

Shout out God's name in your storm! Sing to His name, whatever your circumstances.

BELIEVE HIS NAME FOR YOU

The final thing I want us to catch—and look forward to—is that we will learn more of God's names even in heaven. God bears names we do not yet know. "His eyes are like blazing fire, and on his head are many crowns. He has a *name* written on him that no one knows but he himself" (Revelation 19:12, emphasis mine).

Can you imagine? We will spend all of eternity getting to know this magnificent God and the new names He has!

The book of Revelation speaks to our future name, announcing, "To the one who is victorious, I will give some of the hidden manna. I will also give that person a white stone with a *new name* written on it, known only to the one who receives it" (Revelation 2:17, emphasis mine).

Heaven is for those of us who have been renamed and marked by God. When we overcome and are victorious to the end, God will give us a *new* name in the *new* city where we will live with Him forever. Our new names are important to God right up to the very end!

When we belong to God, we are marked with His name. The author of Revelation writes, "Then I looked, and there before me was the Lamb, standing on Mount Zion, and with him 144,000 who had *his name and his Father's name* written on their foreheads" (Revelation 14:1, emphasis mine).

While this future can seem unbearably far away at times, knowing the new name God has for you today will help you overcome until that time. Remember the incredible name He has given you: "More Than a Conqueror."

God wants to give you a new name that exalts His character. Your new name is meant to highlight Him and the work He has done inside you. You may not feel you have a powerful story, but you have a new name. You bear a story of Him!

Wrapped up in God's names are mysteries about Him that will continue to unfold.

Your new name is an eternal name that no one will be able to take away from you. Seasons change in our lives. Loved ones die. The unexpected happens. Hardships come. We all face loss and opposition, but no matter what, nobody can take away how God has made us new: "The one who is victorious will, like them, be dressed in white. I will never blot out the *name* of that person from

the book of life, but will acknowledge that *name* before my Father
and his angels" (Revelation 3:5, emphasis mine).

Your new name matters to God, and He will call you by it.
Your new name will be recognized by heaven and will go with
you into eternity. Your old labels will not follow you into heaven.
In heaven you will not be identified as "victim" or "less than" or
"inferior" or "insufficient" or "broken."

Believe God's name for you! What has God done inside you?
Your new name will help you overcome and be victorious. One
day, God will wipe every tear from our eyes (Revelation 21:4), and
we will no longer dwell on the pain that came with our old names
and labels. These labels, like "forsaken" and "angry," don't have to
stick with us on earth either. We can forsake the labels that limit
and think of good things instead (Philippians 4:8). We can choose
to dwell on the purity God creates inside us and celebrate how He
has made us new.

Listen to who God says you are and live out of it! Your new
name is evidence that you belong to Him. Living out of your true
name puts His name on display. It's time we start believing what
God has named us and become who He says we are. Let's believe
with our whole selves what has been true from the beginning. Let
us live out of our new names today.

For Further Reflection

Reflection: Have you discovered your new name? What is your favorite name of God? How does God want you to share with others what He has done inside you?

Prayer of Communion: Father, thank You for overcoming the world and making me victorious to the end. Help me to walk with You. Give me courage to walk away from cowardice and continue this journey You have for me. I take refuge in You and have nothing without You. Allow me to hear the new name You have for me and to live it out according to Your might. I want to know Your name and give You the love You are deserving of. Help me to hear, believe, and live out of my new name. You are my beloved God, and I love being Your child. Seal the things You have taught us. Thank You for Jesus. It is in His name we pray. Amen.

Verses to Believe: Psalm 79:9; Matthew 7:7–8; Philippians 2:9; 1 John 5:4

Labels That Limit
Circle which of the old labels you have believed about yourself.

Abandoned	Divorced
Absent	Failure
Alone	Fatherless
Angry	Forgotten
Bad Parent	Forsaken
Broken	Inferior

Infertile	Unable to Pay Child Support
Insufficient	Unemployed
Judged	Unfaithful
Less Than	Unwanted
Lost	Victim
Neglectful	Worrier

Your New Name

Circle which of the new names you want to live out of.

Able to Forgive Others	Overcomer
Adopted	Persevering
Believer	Prayerful
Enduring	Protected
Forgiven	Provided For
Helped	Shepherded
Hopeful	Victorious
Loved Daughter/Son	

What Is Your New Name?

Acknowledgments

To my husband, Joel—it's so fitting that you named this book after giving me your last name. Thank you for making me your bride. You are a man of character, integrity, and wisdom. I love you, and I love our life together!

Asa—you are our beloved son and the joy of our lives! You are God's greatest gift to us. I never knew how much I would love being a mom until I locked eyes with you. I love you and hope to make you proud, son.

To our baby on the way—God was doing a new thing inside me as I wrote these words. His answer to our prayers is you. We love you already and can't wait to meet you.

To my friends and family whose stories I shared—I hope I honored you with my words.

To my siblings via adoption—Cindy, Steve, Kaden, Olivia, Christian, Noah, Isaiah, Isabelle, Jonah, Sophia, Micah, Elijah, Mia, Colsen, Joey, Robbie, Anna, J. J., Jordan, Julianna, Josh, Jack, and Jude—you have given me unconditional love, laughter, and support. God used you to help heal me and give me hope. May you know God's love and my love always.

Zondervan team—you have made this entire publishing process a dream. Thank you.

Stephanie—you are a gifted writer, yet you spend your days fulfilling the dreams of other authors. Thank you for first seeing the vision for this book and for believing I could do it.

Margot—thank you for helping me on this writing journey.

Your expertise brought clarity to this project, and your efficiency helped lighten my load every step of the way.

Lisa—thank you for navigating the changing seasons of life with me.

Nancy Allen—thank you for traveling with me during the first book launch. I will always be grateful to you and Brad for your support and prayers. What an honor it is to be an Allen!

Dear friends—Jennifer Brumm, Kate Wells, Deb Rydman, Amye Olivero, Joe and Joyce Jackson, Del Tackett, Paul and Tammy Rohrbaugh, Stephanie Kelly, Tiffany Kern, Jossie Stern, Megan Maxwell, Jessica Graydon, Rachael Booth, Jim and Heather Essian, Samantha Golden, Cara and Spencer Thompson, Lauren McAfee, Elisha Krauss, Gary Schneeberger, Anne MacDonald, Rachael and Larry Crabb—thank you for your wisdom and supportive friendship.

Thank you to our friends and family who traveled to be with us on our wedding day and at our receptions. Thank you, Mike and Sue Meyerand and Sarah Davis, for your wedding gifts that helped me feel like a bride.

To the readers of *No More Faking Fine*—thank you for carrying this message with courage and lamenting. Your "ending the pretending" stories have given me great hope and courage.

To Andy Stanley and the endorsers of *Your New Name*—your names are worth more than gold. Thank you for lending your name to this book.

To my biological grandma Eleanor "Ellie" Fleece—thank you for teaching me that we're never too old and it's never too late to say "I'm sorry." I love you and miss you.

To my heavenly Father—thank You for finding me, saving me, and naming me. I pray it is Your name that is remembered throughout my life. You are my first love—forever.

Notes

1. *"Kainos,"* HELPS Word-studies, https://bibleapps.com/greek/2537
   .htm.
2. Adapted from Christine's Facebook post, January 30, 2017, https://
   www.facebook.com/theChristineCaine/posts/10158290512690089.
3. Judy Douglass, "The Names God Calls Me," Kindling blog, March
   6, 2013, https://judydouglass.com/blog/2013/03/the-names-god
   -calls-me.
4. See Louie Giglio, *Not Forsaken: Finding Freedom as Sons & Daughters
   of a Perfect Father* (Nashville: B&H, 2019).
5. See Sigal Zohar, "This Week's Question: "Does Jacob Mean 'Deceiver'?"
   eTeacher Biblical, http://eteacherbiblical.com/questions-of-the-week/
   does-jacob-mean-"deceiver".
6. R. C. Sproul, "From Jacob to Israel," *Tabletalk Magazine*, Ligonier
   Ministries, www.ligonier.org/learn/devotionals/jacob-israel.
7. Herbert Lockyer, *All the Women of the Bible* (Grand Rapids: Zondervan,
   1967), 155, www.biblegateway.com/resources/all-women-bible/Sarah
   -Sarai-Sara.
8. Eugene H. Peterson, *Run with the Horses: The Quest for Life at Its Best*
   (Downers Grove, IL: InterVarsity, 1983), 27.
9. Peterson, *Run with the Horses*, 28.
10. Peterson, *Run with the Horses*, 32.
11. John C. Lennox, *Against the Flow: The Inspiration of Daniel in an Age
    of Relativism* (Oxford: Monarch, 2015), 1.
12. Chris Hodges, *The Daniel Dilemma: How to Stand Firm and Love Well
    in a Culture of Compromise* (Nashville: Nelson, 2017), 8.
13. Jen Wilkin, *None Like Him: 10 Ways God Is Different from Us (and Why
    That's a Good Thing)* (Wheaton, IL: Crossway, 2016).

About the Author

Esther Fleece Allen is an accomplished speaker and writer with a heart for helping people overcome adversity. She is passionate about connecting people around the world to practical, faith-centered tools for living through every season, whether it is marked by trial or triumph.

Through the setbacks and celebrations of her own life—many of which she described in her bestselling book, *No More Faking Fine: Ending the Pretending*—she resonates with men and women at all stages of life.

CNN has called Esther one of "Five Women to Watch in Religion," *USA Today* has named her one of the "New Faces of Evangelicalism," and *Christianity Today* listed her as "One of the Top Women Shaping the Church and Culture."

Her insights into the aspirations of millennials have appeared in the *Washington Post* and on CNN, as well as in Barna Group president David Kinnaman's book *You Lost Me: Why Young Christians Are Leaving Church . . . and Rethinking Faith*. She is also the subject of an I Am Second video (www.iamsecond.com/seconds/esther-fleece) documenting her remarkable grace journey.

Esther has a bachelor of arts degree in communications from Oakland University, is a graduate of the Oxford Centre for Christian Apologetics, and is currently in seminary.

Over the past few years, Esther has been given her favorite new names of "Wife" and "Mother." When she's not traveling to speak or teach, she enjoys being at home with her husband and children. Keep up with her growing family and global adventures at estherfleeceallen.com.

No More Faking Fine

Ending the Pretending

Esther Fleece

If you've ever been given empty clichés during challenging times, you know how painful it can feel to be misunderstood by well-meaning people. Far too often, it seems the response we get to our hurt and disappointment is to suck it up, or pray it away.

But Scripture reveals a God who meets us where we are, not where we pretend to be.

No More Faking Fine is your invitation to get gut-level honest with God through the life-giving language of lament. Lament, a practice woven throughout Scripture, is a prayer that God never ignores, never silences, and never wastes. As author Esther Fleece Allen says, "Lament is the unexpected pathway to true intimacy with God, and with those around us."

Esther learned this the hard way by believing she could shut down painful emotions that haunted her from a broken past she tried to forget on her fast track to success. But in silencing her pain, she robbed herself of the opportunity to be healed. Maybe you've done the same.

No More Faking Fine is your permission to lament—to give voice to the hurt, frustration, and disappointment you've kept inside and silenced for too long. Drawing from careful biblical study and hard-won insight, Esther reveals how to use God's own language to draw closer to Him as He leads us through any darkness into His marvelous light.

Available in stores and online!